Oh! Mr. Porter . . . she isn't going to Birmingham on the Wirral Railway, but perhaps for a day out at New Brighton. A light-hearted moment at Liscard & Poulton station in days when ankles were not permitted to be seen! (Photo: J. Ryan collection).

Steel Wheels to Deeside

The Wirral Railway past and present

by

John W. Gahan

Cover Design: ERIC R. MONKS

By the same author:

Seventeen Stations to Dingle — the L 'erpool Overhead Railway remembered.

The Line Beneath the Liners — A hundred years of Mersey Railway sights and sounds.

First published 1983 by Countyvise Limited, 1 & 3 Grove Road, Rock Ferry, Birkenhead, Merseyside L42 3XS . . . .
. . . . **ISBN 0 907768 70 9**
and

Avon AngliA Publications & Services, Annesley House, 21 Southside, Weston-super-Mare, Avon BS23 2QU . . . .
. . . . **ISBN 0 905466 61 6**

Copyright © John W. Gahan, 1983
Photoset and Printed by Birkenhead Press Limited, 1 & 3 Grove Road, Rock Ferry, Birkenhead, Wirral, Merseyside L42 3XS.

FOREWORD

The present-day Wirral Lines of Merseyrail, with their busy and frequent train services, had very humble beginnings in the 60's of the last century, when optimistic promoters had a single line railway built between Wallasey Bridge Road and Hoylake with the hope of developing the then wild and sparsely populated Northern extremity of the Wirral Peninsular. Success did not at first crown their efforts, for the little railway soon became impoverished and had the distinction of having part of it seized by bailiffs. After a fresh start under different management in 1872, the system began to develop, as did the countryside it served, with steam traction giving way to electrification in 1938.

This book is not the complete history of the Wirral Railway, for there is no doubt that much remains to be researched and recorded. The intention is to provide briefly, the story of what are now the Wirral Lines of Merseyrail with the hope that it will appeal to those who knew the system during the steam era, and also interest present-day passengers most of whom will have known it only since electrification.

The "Wirral" was a well-loved railway, for it took people to work and carried many thousands to enjoy sunny days on the sands at Hoylake, Moreton, West Kirby and New Brighton, and many hikers who struck off into the country from intermediate stations. May its memory remain green in the minds of all railway devotees and the people who worked on it, and with all good will to those who operate it today in very different circumstances than of old.

Liverpool,
July, 1983.

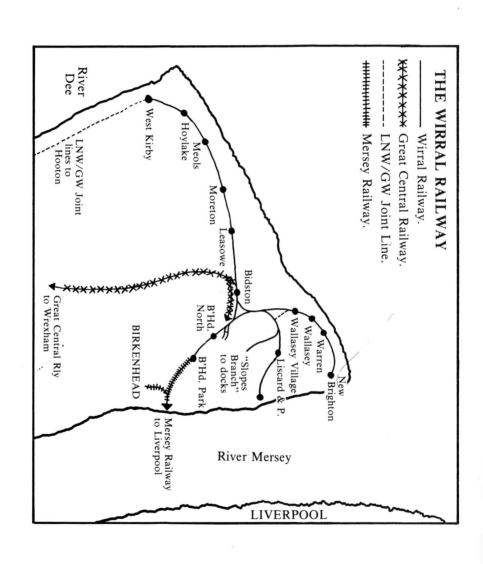

THE WIRRAL RAILWAY

——— Wirral Railway.
✖✖✖✖✖✖✖ Great Central Railway.
— — — LNW/GW Joint Line.
╫╫╫╫╫╫╫╫╫ Mersey Railway.

River Dee

West Kirby

Hoylake

Meols

Moreton

Leasowe

LNW/GW Joint lines to Hooton

Bidston

Great Central Rly to Wrexham

B'Hd. North

BIRKENHEAD

B'Hd. Park

"Slopes Branch" to docks

Wallasey Village

Wallasey

Warren

Liscard & P.

New Brighton

Mersey Railway to Liverpool

River Mersey

LIVERPOOL

Rusting Rails over Drifting Sands

The district known as "The Wirral" in North West Cheshire, is the broad peninsular that lies between the silted-up River Dee of the sandbanks and the busy dock-lined River Mersey. For centuries a large part of the pleasant rural peninsular was used for farming and agricultural purposes but with the rise of the port of Liverpool and later Birkenhead, it began to assume the role of residential dormitory for the lords of commerce and later still, a holiday rendezvous for the populace of both towns, and has been subjected to enormous development, both residential and industrial over the last century or so. Consisting of approximately 130 square miles, the Wirral is flat and marshy at its North Western extremity with sand hills along the seaward coast, whilst the remainder is undulating country with a few modest heights such as parts of Wallasey, Tranmere, Bidston Hill, Thurstaston and Caldy Hills and the uplands know as Heswall Hills.

Prior to the 1820's there was little or no industry in the Wirral, only small villages existing on farming, whilst those on the coast sustained themselves mainly by fishing. An exception however was Parkgate, on the River Dee, which was once a thriving little port, but any development that might have materialised was thwarted by the silting of the river eventually isolating the port from the sea and now only sand, mud and crab grass meet the gaze where once small but sturdy sailing ships tied up at the quayside or rode at anchor offshore. The once busy quay has not seen a ship for many ages and for years has formed part of a pleasant promenade which, with the riverside buildings has plenty of olde worlde charm.

Birkenhead, of shipbuilding fame, only began to develop in the 1850's when William Laird, who had established a shipyard and iron foundry on the shores of Wallasey Pool moved his business to the West bank of the River Mersey. Other industries too, were established around the Pool, which was a creek of the Mersey which penetrated inland for a considerable distance, and formed the nucleus of the extensive Birkenhead and Wallasey dock system, becoming known as the Great Float. Grandiose plans were formulated by Laird and others for what was to be a magnificent city, laid out on the grid system with long, straight and wide streets. A start was made on this venture with the construction of Hamilton Square, the splendid and dignified buildings of which gave some indication of the glories to come. Alas however, the dream faded and this early example of town planning ran out of steam. The plans were largely abandoned so the town developed haphazardly, only a few streets being built on the grid system. Birkenhead thus became a busy place of shipyards, docks and various industrial plants, with instead of grand Georgian mansions, street after street of small terraced houses to accommodate the work forces. Housing standards and street design became much better as the town expanded outwards however.

To the North of Birkenhead lay the district which became known as Wallasey, formed by the villages of Seacombe, Poulton and Liscard, with Egremont and New Brighton being newer places added later. Development in this area consisted of docks, grain mills and other industries on the North side of the Pool, with residential districts expanding gradually so that the once isolated villages eventually became part of an extensive connurbation. It was the introduction of ferry services on the River Mersey which gave the development of Wallasey its greatest impetus, putting it in quick and direct communication with Liverpool. Birkenhead too, had its ferry services which were actually very much older than those of Wallasey.

After the opening of the Chester & Birkenhead Railway in 1840, there was little scope for further railways in Wirral, or so it seemed, and 26 years elapsed before any move was made towards the construction of more lines on the peninsular, the possibilities of residential development providing the motive for the next episode in its railway history.

During the early 1860's a body known as the Hoylake Railway Company was formed by a group of far-sighted (or optimistic) gentlemen led by a former railway official — Braithwaite Poole, who had for some years been the Goods Manager at the L&NWR Waterloo Dock station, Liverpool. They proposed to construct a railway across the flat, marshy and sparsely populated Northern extremity of the Wirral Peninsular, in order to connect Birkenhead with the fishing village of Hoylake with the intention of opening up the land for residential purposes in much the same way that the Liverpool-Southport railway had developed similar terrain on the Lancashire side of the Mersey.

The company applied for Parliamentary Powers to build a line between Seacombe (instead of Birkenhead as originally intended) and Hoylake, via Poulton and Bidston, with a branch from the latter place to Wallasey Bridge Road in order to serve Birkenhead Docks. The Parliamentary Bill was passed on 28th July, 1863 and construction of the railway was duly commenced. As events turned out, Seacombe did not become the terminus, nor was it even served by the railway until many years later. The line, as constructed ran from Wallasey Bridge Road to Hoylake and consisted of a single track only. Apart from problems caused by sand, no difficulties were met with during construction. T .e Chief Engineer for the line was Benjamin Piercy, the chairman being J. Everitt.

The completed railway was inspected by Captain Ritchie on behalf of the Board of Trade on Saturday, 16th June 1866 and it was opened to traffic without any ceremony on the following Monday, 18th June. Commencement of operations was announced to the public by the following brief notice which appeared in the "Liverpool Mercury";

8

HOYLAKE RAILWAY – This Railway is NOW OPEN to the public for general traffic.
BRAITHWAITE POOLE General Manager,
5 Jackson Chambers, Castle Street,
June 18th 1866.

Not withstanding this notice, regular train services did not commence until 2nd July, 1866. Connection between Seacombe Ferry and the railway was provided by Mr. Thomas Evans, a coach and omnibus proprietor, who operated a vehicle which ran in conjunction with the trains, but the initial train service was a sparse one of six each way on weekdays and four on Sundays. This service was actually reduced for a time subsequently!

The Hoylake Railway attracted few passengers after the initial novelty had worn off and soon began to lose money. From the very start Braithwaite Poole and his fellow directors not only had this to worry about — they also felt the sharp quills of the "Porcupine", a weekly Liverpool journal, the editor of which featured the misfortunes of the railway several times in his columns. For instance, the edition of 14th July, 1866, contained the following:-

GREAT PUFFS & SLOW RETURNS
"Who in Liverpool, has not heard of our Admirable Chrichton —
Mr. Braithwaite Poole — equally famous and ever ready with his pen, be the subject philosophical, theological or mere business – par et simple? After being for some time presiding genius of the London and Northwestern Railway, the directors of that 'bloated' concern suddenly discovered that their brilliant Poole had kicked off the dust of his shoes against them, and left his chair of state at the Waterloo station to be filled by some more commonplace individual. On this, the Great Western Company – thinking to profit by the fatuity of their rival – eagerly offered a good 'sit' to the brilliant B.P.; but here again an untoward fate once more obliged him to resign his situation. The great railway directors were evidently against Mr. Poole – so much the worse for the great railway directors, though their lines still apparently manage to drag on an existence somehow. In this conjuncture, some astute people doubtless said to themselves 'It's quite evident that jealous directors and rival officials won't give our friend Poole a fair chance, so he shall have a new railway all to himself and then he'll confound his directors and astonish the public!" So a railway was forthwith commenced to unite Hoylake to Liverpool and the press was cleverly 'tooled' to vaunt the praises of the new railway. The line was to be the cheapest, the carriages the finest and the management the most perfect in the world and the Sands of Hoylake were to be brought within half-an-hour of the Exchange Flags. At least, so said in chorus the weekly and daily press of Liverpool and Cheshire, not forgetting sly little 'puffs insiduous' in London and provincial papers. At last, after several delays and

9

one false start, the Hoylake Railway is opened and so far, for any good it is to the hard-worked, dust-choked dweller in Liverpool, the line might just have well remained original soil. The few trains run at long and inconvenient intervals, and the last train from Hoylake – in July, mind you – leaves at 7 p.m., about the hour when an ordinary business man might expect to join his family at dinner or tea – according to his tastes or social standing. So, after all the columns of puffing, this 'Model Railway' – managed by the great Braithwaite Poole – comes to this. Already the public discontent is loud and general and unless something like a rational time-table is arranged and kept to, Mr. Poole and his directors will find that something more than erratic genius is required to make a railway paying and popular".

The Hoylake Railway was a little over five miles in length — a slender thread of iron which at that time had little prospect of lucrative traffic in the thinly populated district which it bravely traversed. The company was short of money and could not afford new locomotives and rolling stock. Operations were commenced with two locomotives and a few four-wheeled carriages of spartan comfort, all second hand, and with a great deal of mileage already to their credit. Braithwaite Poole, whose last position prior to forming the Hoylake Railway Company was that of General Manager of the Wallasey Ferries, seems to have been the Hoylake Railway in person, at first as Secretary, then General Manager — he certainly dominated the company's activities and worked ceaselessly to promote the line. One of his more notable characteristics was boundless optimism which was not shared by the editor of the "Porcupine"! The latter faced facts however — there was little traffic and slender hope of financial success while the railway reached neither the shores of the Mersey or Dee. Poole was destined to enjoy a short career at the head of his enterprise, for the railway soon fell on evil days. It was only after proper connections with Birkenhead were established that the railway began to be renumerative, but this took place under different management. The company were nevertheless ambitious — even before the railway was opened they had completed plans for various extensions but possessed no funds to carry them out. A branch from Bidston to New Brighton was authorised by a Parliamentary Act of 5th July, 1865 and on 16th July, 1866 Powers were granted for an extension from Hoylake to West Kirby, plus a further extension along the East bank of the River Dee to Neston. The West Kirby and New Brighton lines did not materialise in the Poole regime however, and neither did the proposed Neston extension, that village being reached by the London & North Western and Great Western Joint Railways by their line from Hooton which was later extended to West Kirby.

The most ambitious of the Hoylake company's schemes was that for an extension into North Wales, crossing the wide estuary of the River Dee, which would have entailed the construction of a viaduct about seven miles in length, with a swing span on the Welsh side to allow vessels to reach Connah's Quay. Needless to say, the company had no hope of embarking on this project and it remained an unrealised dream. In recent times motoring interests have called for such a bridge and it is a fairly safe bet that few of those whose voices are raised in this cause realise that the idea of spanning the Dee estuary is a very old one indeed! Nevertheless, such a bridge will no doubt materialise in due course to provide a much-needed short cut between Liverpool and North Wales, but it is unlikely to carry a railway track.

The first few weeks that the Hoylake railway was in operation saw a reasonable amount of passenger traffic, but this was not maintained and as many head-shaking onlookers had predicted, the receipts began to fall far short of expectations. Nevertheless, the directors put on a show of optimism that did not fool everybody, least of all the redoubtable editor of "The Porcupine", who, watching events closely was motivated to pen the following in the edition of 17th November, 1866 . . . .

WELL, I NEVER!
"A meeting of the Hoylake Railway company was held on Tuesday, when a report was read in which it was stated that 'the traffic has been regularly and efficiently conducted' and further 'that the result is encouraging'. Now, is not this a trifle too congratulatory? If these remarks are true, what about the indignation meetings at Moreton and elsewhere? What about the constant complaints of paucity of trains, especially at night? Furthermore, what about the gross muddle at the last Hoylake races? The results may be very encouraging to directors and secretaries; but we fancy shareholders and the travelling public will not endorse this 'flattering tale' ".

Not only did the Hoylake Railway Company suffer from poor financial returns but a greater misfortune befell them. They were the victims of a financial crash which affected several other concerns also, this being due to the collapse of the bankers, Overend & Gurney Ltd. In the event they found themselves in a serious situation before very long, which cut their railway short and gave them even less opportunity to prosper. A local land owner, Mr. Vyner, of Bidston, through whose territory the railway passed was apparently not paid for some land and therefore instructed his bailiffs to seize the section of line between Wallasey Bridge Road and Leasowe, which they duly did and operations on this stretch were suspended. This unfortunate situation provided further ammunition for the literary artillery of the "The Porcupine's" editor, who promptly fired another volley at the luckless company in the following words which appeared in the edition of 25th September, 1869:-

RAILROAD TO RUIN

"If Mr. Boucicault feels inclined to 'do' a comic drama on the subject of railways – which somehow seemed to tickle his fancy – he will find a good subject for his muse in the history and misfortune of the Hoylake Railway. Being a pet scheme and hobby of our local Admirable Crichton – the versatile Braithwaite Poole – it ought to have succeeded! But somehow it has only served to prove to credulous share-holders that the hobbies of the cleverest Pooles may lead to bottomless pits for their funds. So far, the entire concern has only served as a joke to those who did not own it; and the rolling stock has been little else than a laughing stock to all who have had to travel on the flattest and dullest railway ever imagined or constructed.

The climax of the "Hoylake's" misfortunes appears to have now arrived; and Mr. Vyner, the lord of the manor, who says he was never paid for his land has seized portions of the luckless line and sold it by auction. The sale itself, was of course, not a success and the whole affair appears likely to find its terminus in the Court of Chancery – a Terminus where funds once locked up are apt to remain stationary and whence the return tickets are very few indeed. Wonderful thing steam, sir, says the bore of a railway carriage; but some of its wonders are the reverse of pleasant when they lead to collisions and drive a host of deluded shareholders into the ruinous quagmires of liquidation. Ropes of sand have hitherto been considered the very ideals of useless industry but railways on sand which lead from nowhere in particular to nowhere in general appear to be just as unprofitable – especially when built on land that is not paid for. At all events, the Hoylake Railway points one moral – that, to pay, a railway should have termini in populous localities, be cheaply made, well managed and useful to other people than the employees".

The Hoylake Railway Company became bankrupt in 1869 but business did not completely cease however. Only the section of the railway seized by Mr. Vyner, that between Wallasey Bridge Road and Leasowe appears to have been devoid of traffic for the period from 31st December, 1869 to 31st July, 1872. The future of the remainder (Leasowe to Hoylake) seemed to be decidedly bleak, but it was kept going pending a solution of the problems being experienced. Rescue eventually came however, from Birkenhead, in the form of a newly constituted body entitled the Hoylake & Birkenhead Rail and Tramway Company, which was granted Parliamentary Powers on 1st July, 1872, to construct tramways in the streets of Birkenhead and also to take over and re-open the Hoylake Railway throughout. The company set to work on the task of revival of the moribund railway and re-introduced full train services on 1st August. Between the date of the seizure and the re-opening, a train service had been provided only between Leasowe level crossing (there was no station there then) and Hoylake, with road coach connections to and from Birkenhead and Seacombe.

Wirral Railway No.1, a 4-4-2 Tank engine built in 1892. Withdrawn from service for scrap in 1924. It was allotted LMS No.6830. (Photo: J. Ward collection).

Seacombe, Hoylake & Deeside Railway 2-4-0 Tank engine No.3. Built in 1884 and withdrawn in 1914. (Photo: J.W. Gahan collection).

A train for West Kirby at Hoylake station, circa 1890. The engine is 0-4-4 Tank No.8, built in 1887 and withdrawn in 1923. (Photo: J. Ward collection).

One of the large Wirral Railway 0-6-4 Tank engines, No.12, stands alongside the well-known 'zeppelin' water tank at Birkenhead North. This locomotive was built in 1900, and lasted until 1924. It was allotted LMS number.6948. (Photo: J. Ward collection).

New Life and New Prospects

No developments took place between 1872 and 1877, but during 1878 the very necessary extension from Hoylake to West Kirby was completed and opened on 1st April. On that date also a short connecting line between Wallasey Bridge Road station and the docks railway (the latter having connections with the L&NW and GW Railways) was opened for goods traffic. The company also constructed a street tramway between Wallasey Bridge Road and Woodside Ferry, Birkenhead, this being opened in 1873. It was of course, worked by horses, not mechanical power. On 11th October, 1879 this tramway was sold to another concern, the Birkenhead Tramway Company.

Braithwaite Poole left the Hoylake railway in 1870 and set himself up in business as an arbitrator for railways, with an office at No. 22 Brown's Buildings, Exchange, Liverpool, but moved to No. 35 in the same building during 1874. He seems to have ceased business soon after the latter date, for he is listed as a 'Gentleman' in the 1875 Directory, residing in Claughton, Birkenhead. Few of the millions of passengers who enjoy today's highly efficient train services in the Wirral have heard of Braithwaite Poole, who, with his fellow directors were the unsung pioneers of one of the country's most successful railways notwithstanding early failures and shortcomings — Poole's dreams were realised a hundredfold long after his decease.

By an act of 18th July, 1881, the name of the company was changed, being no longer relevant after disposal of the tramways, and it became known by the less cumbersome title of Seacombe, Hoylake & Deeside Railway. This title was slightly inaccurate however, because Seacombe was not yet on the railway map. Lack of finance held up developments but the extension to Seacombe continually occupied the minds of the directors because connection with that place would provide the railway with much additional traffic in passengers to and from North-West Wirral, who would use the Mersey ferry steamers with an almost adjacent transfer from train to boat or vice-versa, with no road journey intervening as was still the case for those who used the Woodside ferry and joined the trains at Bridge Road station, Wallasey. Moreover, Seacombe was developing industrially and residentially, and so was a desirable goal, but it remained rail-less for some time longer.

The story now begins to become somewhat complex. On 13th June, 1883 an Act was passed for the formation of the Wirral Railway Company, a concern formed with the object of constructing a railway from the Mersey company's Birkenhead Central station to a point near Woodchurch on the "Dee Extension", the latter being another project of the Wirral Railway Company. This latter line was to run from Bidston to Harwarden Bridge, there to link up with the

Chester-North Wales line of the Manchester, Sheffield & Lincolnshire Railway. The Birkenhead Central scheme did not materialise however being replaced by an alternative line from a point West of Wallasey Bridge Road to Birkenhead Park, with an intermediate station at Birkenhead Docks. At Park station it would meet the Mersey Railway, which was to be extended from Hamilton Square, Birkenhead to meet it. On 14th August, 1884, the Wirral Company were granted powers for a branch line from Bidston to New Brighton, an extension long intended by the Seacombe, Hoylake & Deeside Company, who had so far been unable to build it.

Shortly after the formation of the Wirral Railway Company, another with a similar title — the Wirral Railway Company Limited was created by an Act of the same date that the other company obtained their Act for the New Brighton line. The newer company was empowered to buy the shares of the 1883 Wirral, and SH&D Companies, and to merge them under the title of Wirral Railway, but the latter did not take place until some years later however. The Wirral Railway Co. Ltd. transferred the construction of the Birkenhead Park extension to the Wirral company, whilst Birkenhead Docks station was actually built by the SH&D Company to replace the original station of the Hoylake Railway at Wallasey Bridge Road, the new station and a short length of line leading to it being opened on 2nd January, 1888. While the SH&D Company were engaged on the last named work, the Wirral Company were busy on the Birkenhead Park extension, meeting the Mersey Railway branch from Hamilton Square also under way. All these new lines were brought into use on the same day, 2nd January, 1888. From that date the trains of the Mersey Railway terminated at Birkenhead Park, where passengers changed for the onward journey into Wirral and vice-versa. Through workings, though not by every train were commenced on 1st May, 1890 which obviated the change of trains for passengers, but locomotives were changed at this "frontier" station which became known as "Park" and is still referred to as such today. This through working did not last long, as a disagreement between the two companies caused it to be discontinued on 30th June, 1894, and it was not resumed, even though relations became amiable again in due course. Birkenhead Park became a "Joint" Station, with its own administrative committee, and passengers continued to change trains until the sweeping alterations made many years afterwards in March, 1938, of which more later.

Construction of the New Brighton branch, diverging from the main line a little distance West of Docks station had been proceeding at the same time as the aforementioned works and was opened as far as Grove Road, Wallasey on the same date as the extension to Birkenhead Park (2nd January, 1888), and the remainder on to New Brighton was brought into use on 30th March, 1888. The town of New Brighton, founded as a seaside resort about the year 1830, was becoming increasingly popular and although served by ferries on the Mersey, was not to see extensive development until the railway came. A tall tower, rivalling that of Blackpool was built in 1897, a landmark for miles around that thrust its steelwork into the sky to a height of 562 feet, but had a short life however, for it was taken down during 1920-21. The branch to New Brighton handled a fair residential traffic throughout the year but it put the railway well and truly into the day-trip passenger business during the summer months. The line approached the resort through sand dunes which gave a great deal of trouble to the track maintenance staff when strong winds blew sand over the railway, curving Eastwards at the corner of the peninsula and ran into the North-West end of the town terminating just beyond the "amusement area". Elegantly designed Victorian shops fronted by glazed canopies on iron columns were built in the town and pleasant, large houses were constructed on the perimeter, but the river frontage developed into a hotch-potch of low-class restaurants and amusement arcades that earned it the unbecoming title of the "ham and egg parade". These were later swept away and replaced by pleasant gardens and more elegant buildings. The promenade and sands presented a spectacle of hordes of people jostling for space — men in straw hats and stiff collars, women wearing the lengthy skirts of the era — even the bathers were heavily dressed. Surviving photographs of beach scenes convey the impression that holidaymakers endured rather than enjoyed their hours on the sands! Nevertheless, New Brighton drew the crowds who packed the trains and the paddle steamers on the Mersey.

During 1888 an agreement was concluded whereby the Wirral Railway Company Ltd. took over the operation of the Seacombe, Hoylake & Deeside Railway and later, on 11th June, 1891 the two companies were amalgamated under the title of Wirral Railway Company. This was the realisation of the object for which the former Wirral Railway Company Ltd. had been formed back in 1883. One of the first acts of the new company was to embark on the construction of the Seacombe Branch, a task that involved quite a large amount of engineering work in the making of cuttings and road overbridges to enable the line to persue its sinuous course through the Liscard and Poulton districts to terminate only a few hundred yards from the Seacombe ferry landing, the station being named Seacombe & Egremont. Only one intermediate station was provided, this being named Liscard & Poulton. The branch was opened on 1st June, 1895 — nearly 30 years after it was proposed. Its construction was viewed with acute disfavour by the Mersey Railway Company, which was at that time losing money and needless to say, feared further losses through the possibility of people using the new route as a means of travelling to and from Wirral stations and Liverpool instead of using their own line, but they really had little to fear because the ferry voyage between Liverpool and Seacombe was a much slower business than riding on the Mersey Railway between Liverpool and

Birkenhead Park. The Seacombe route did not achieve popularity among any but day trippers bent on visiting the beaches or countryside and those residents of the Poulton and Liscard districts of Wallasey, who were employed in Liverpool — relatively few at that date. It did however, carry considerable goods and coal traffic.

The construction of the New Brighton and Seacombe Branches resulted in the formation of two triangular junctions on Bidston Moss, an extensive low-lying marshy expanse. That nearest Bidston was controlled by three signal boxes — Bidston East Junction, Bidston West Junction and Bidston North Junction. The other triangular junction was nearer to Wallasey and was known as Seacombe Junction, which also had a signal box at each extremity; Seacombe Junction No.1 at the South end. No.2 at the East end and No.3 at the North end. The Easterly section of the latter triangle enabled the company to introduce a local passenger train service between Seacombe and New Brighton which, becoming known locally as "The Dodger" ran only during the summer to cater for holidaymakers. The service was a round-about one however and was subject to severe competition from the Wallasey Council Tramways and was discontinued in 1911. The rails were removed from the Eastern section of the triangle in 1916, during the Great War, and shipped to France for military use. The formation, which could be traced until recently was left derelict. In the centre of this triangular junction there was a pond that was once part of the Western extremity of Wallasey Pool, into which ran the narrow River Fender which the railway crosses. The pond was a favourite venue for young anglers. It was incredible to realise that this small expanse of water was part of the vast expanse only a little distance away, on which ocean-going ships sailed almost into the countryside, for Wallasey Pool formed the nucleus of Birkenhead and Wallasey docks.

The main line of the Wirral Railway was of course, that between Birkenhead Park and West Kirby. Before it was doubled train operation was carried out on the staff and ticket system and crossing loops were provided at Moreton and Hoylake — these were however, built only when the line was extended to West Kirby. The single line had become an operating headache by the early 1890's, so, in 1894 the work of installing a second track was put in hand and completed to Hoylake by June, 1895. A station was built at Leasowe as part of this improvement programme. At the West Kirby end of the line negotiations were begun for provision of a "joint" station, to be shared by the Wirral and LNWR/GWR systems, with through train working over the latter companies' jointly operated branch from Hooton that also terminated at West Kirby, which had by then become a small seaside resort of the more genteel and quiet kind. The negotiations came to nought however, so the Wirral company retained their own independent station, which they rebuilt in 1898-9. The L&NW/GW companies built their own station almost "next door" to that of the Wirral Company.

For a time before the 1914-1918 war the Wirral company ran excursion trains over the Hooton branch between West Kirby and Parkgate. For a much longer period however, goods trains worked from Hooton to Birkenhead Docks and vice-versa via West Kirby and the Wirral line and this practice continued well into the years of British Railways after Nationalisation.

The foregoing completes the list of "main" lines that formed the Wirral Railway at its maximum extent. The company operated frequent train services which catered for an ever-expanding residential district, the gorse covered sand-lands and green fields that bordered the line gradually becoming built over as time passed, at first near the stations, latterly elsewhere with the development of motors and bus services. On 1st January, 1923 the Wirral Railway became part of the vast London, Midland & Scottish Railway system and its individual, local character inevitably vanished as standardisation made itself felt, though this was a gradual process.

There remains to be mentioned the subsequent fate of the Wirral Railway Company's line between Bidston and Hawarden Bridge, for which Powers had been granted on 31st December, 1885, the work to be carried out under the auspices of the other Wirral Company. Work was put in hand on construction of the line but the money ran out and they could not finish the task. The Powers were thereupon transferred to the Manchester, Sheffield & Lincolnshire and the Wrexham, Mold & Connah's Quay Railway Companies jointly, under the Wirral Railway Company's Transfer Act of 12th May, 1889. The line, known as The North Wales & Liverpool Railway was duly completed, but the Wirral Company had no further interest in it except in the matter of Running Powers for MS&L (later Great Central) and WM&CQ trains over the Seacombe Branch. The WM&CQ trains ran to Seacombe from 1896 but the MS&L trains did not work through beyond Bidston until 1898.

We have already noted the nature of the terrain through which the Wirral Railway persued its course — a mixture of agricultural and grazing land, with marshes and sand dunes along the North West coast of the peninsula. The ever-drifting sand was a constant source of trouble in the early days of the line. Indeed, on 29th September, 1866 the locomotive of the 5.15 p.m. train from Hoylake was derailed by a sand drift near the latter place and became bogged down and, as there was no other engine available the train was cancelled. The next train out, the 7.15 p.m. had to be hauled by horses in ignominious fashion while the errant steam locomotive remained embedded in the sand!

On the New Brighton line drifts often buried the rails completely and gangs of men had to be called out to shovel the sand into wagons for removal. Sand screens were erected eventually, but it was not until after the line had become part of the London, Midland &

Scottish Railway that the sand menace was taken firmly in hand, that company having gorse and starr grass planted on the dunes which effectively prevented the myriads of grains from encroaching on the track. The sandy nature of the ground made for very quiet running of the trains however. In recent times the sand dunes have been almost entirely removed.

To the locomotive department sand was a menace that taxed them to the full, and removing it from the oily surface of slide bars and motion rods was an essential task to prevent abrasion and seizure, as the engines were constantly exposed to wind-driven sand until the trouble was cured.

Drifting sand was a menace to operations on the New Brighton line, as shown here as a train traverses the coastal section of line near Wallasey (Grove Road) station. The engine is 0-6-4 Tank No.12. (Photo: J. Ryan collection).

View Westwards from Bidston station, September, 1964. Today the M53 motorway blights this scene, whilst all the sidings and GC lines have been removed. (Photo: J.W. Gahan).

View Eastwards from Bidston station in September, 1964. The branch to Seacombe diverges to the left. The former Great Central Railway lines are on the right hand side. (Photo J.W. Gahan).

21

A Wintry scene at Leasowe station in Wirral Railway days. Note the primitive signal with the spectacle glasses separate from the semaphore arm. The levers for working the signals and crossing gates were housed in the tin shack at the platform end. (Photo: J. Ryan collection).

The well-known Meols Pond on the South side of Meols station,, as it appeared in the Spring of 1983. (Photo: S.G. Jones).

Moreton station with the adjacent shanty town, circa 1923. Cadbury's biscuit factory now covers the site of the bungalows. The locomotive is a former L&NWR 0-6-2 "Coal Tank", several of which were sent to the Wirral line shortly after the railway Grouping. (Photo: J. Ryan collection).

HOYLAKE STATION

Hoylake station, looking towards Birkenhead in 1906. Passengers await the 1.00 p.m. train, whilst a locomotive shunts wagons in the sidings. All the buildings shown were swept away when the station was rebuilt in 1937. (Photo: J. Ryan collection).

The approaches to West Kirby station. On the left-hand side, the fire station now occupies the site of the former goods and coal yard. May, 1983. (Photo: S.G. Jones).

The exterior of West Kirby station has altered little since it was built, and, except for the signs and parked cars, this 1983 scene looks more or less the same as in Wirral Railway days. (Photo: S.G. Jones).

The Railway and its Features

The main line between Birkenhead Park and West Kirby had intermediate stations at Birkenhead Docks (later re-named North) Bidston, Leasowe, Meols, Moreton and Hoylake. All were tiny places when the railway was built and all have grown enormously, some out of all recognition in subsequent years. All the intermediate stations except Birkenhead Docks were primitive in form, consisting of timber-faced cinder platforms with small shelters of wood or corrugated iron. They remained basically in this condition until the late 1930's. Goods and coal yards with sidings were provided at all stations except Leasowe and Meols. Hoylake had carriage sidings and a spur serving the gas works, whilst a siding served the Moreton brick works. A new station was built at Manor Road, Hoylake in 1938 but this had no goods facilities. On the New Brighton Branch there were three intermediate stations, the largest being Wallasey Grove Road, built of red bricks, spacious and well designed. Wallasey Village, (opened in 1907) is a simple station with no architectural merits. The remaining station was at Warren between Grove Road and New Brighton, having cinder platforms and corrugated iron shelters. Warren was closed in 1917 and gradually disappeared under the sand. Its passengers were mainly people proceeding to the nearby links to play golf.

On the Seacombe Branch the only intermediate station was Liscard & Poulton, an island platform with simple timber buildings. The Seacombe terminus was fairly primitive, consisting of corrugated iron and timber huts and cinder platforms, these being an island and a single platform on the South side. Extensive sidings and connections with the dock railways were laid down in the vicinity of Bidston and Poulton, whilst sidings served the Wallasey Gas and Electricity works. Seacombe had a large goods and coal yard with several sidings.

Bidston, Liscard & Poulton, West Kirby and New Brighton stations had island type platforms with rails either side. At West Kirby a Yard and several sidings intervened between the Wirral Railway station and that of the L&NWR/GWR "next door", so that passengers changing trains had to walk between the two via the public road. No stations on the whole of the system were situated on enbankments and only Birkenhead Park, Birkenhead North and Liscard & Poulton were in cuttings. Level crossings exist at Bidston, Leasowe and Hoylake. Elsewhere roads cross the line on bridges except at Wallasey Village, at which the roadway was lowered to pass beneath the railway, replacing a former level crossing. Numerous unmanned occupation crossings took minor roads and cart tracks across the railway on the Bidston-West Kirby section and some of these still remain in use.

The main line between Birkenhead Park and West Kirby runs in a generally Westerly direction, curving gradually South-Westwards beyond Meols and is more or less level all the way, the gradients where such exist being only slight. The first station reached after leaving Birkenhead North is Bidston, which is overlooked at a distance by Bidston Hill with its Observatory and old windmill. For most of its life this station, situated about half-a-mile from the village, has been in an open windswept location, there being but a few cottages near it until late Victorian times when Station Road, on the South side of the railway became subject to development and a number of fine, large houses built, which still survive, but the road in the vicinity of the station was bordered by fields until very recently. On the North side of the line a narrow lane led to farmyards and golf links, with open fields stretching away towards the coast, whilst to the North-East Bidston Moss, a vast area of low-lying land stretched away towards Wallasey. This area became flooded nearly every winter, a footpath alongside the railway often being submerged and many a youthful train watcher got wet and muddy feet! This trouble was taken in hand in recent years and the flooding largely eliminated.

Electrification, which took place in 1938 and of which more later, hardly altered the character of this pleasant station, built in true "Wirral" style with cinders and timber platforms and two separate timber huts for office and waiting rooms etc. The platforms were raised, concrete-faced and resurfaced for the electrification but the timber huts remain today, connected by a timber screen and canopy to provide extra shelter for passengers, this amenity also having been added at the time of electrification. The old atmosphere lingered at Bidston station as it did at no other until the late 1960's when not only the character of the station but of its surroundings underwent vast changes through industrial and road-building developments — the rural peace has gone forever!

The most noticeable feature of Bidston station is its lengthy footbridge, a concrete structure that replaced an aged and latterly somewhat dilapidated timber footbridge in June, 1963. A level crossing over which four tracks passed (two former Wirral and two Great Central) still exists at the East end of the station. The gates were not controlled by the signal box, which is at the West end of the station, but by a ground frame. Until the recent developments the road that passed over the crossing led to a farm and golf links and saw relatively little traffic. Any motorist wishing to cross the lines gave a blast or two on his car horn, upon which the station porter would emerge from his office and operate the gates. Passengers use the footbridge to enter and leave the station and do not cross the line. The open footbridge is no place to linger in the Winter, being in an exposed position with nothing to break the force of the wind that sweeps across the fields of Wirral.

A small yard with two widely separated sidings was situated on the South side of the line. The outer siding was mainly used for domestic coal traffic, the other being occupied by the Central Wagon Company of Wigan, who maintained a small repair shop in the yard until 1964. Since withdrawal of coal and goods traffic at Bidston, which took place in 1968, the two sidings were used by the Engineering Department and the yard itself used as a store for equipment. These sidings were however, removed during 1981, rather surprisingly in view of their usefulness. A dead-end refuge siding existed on the North (Up) side of Bidston station, but this saw little use and was usually overgrown with weeds, its rails being dark with rust and saw little, if any, use in latter years. The points for this siding were at the East end of the station, near the level crossing. As there was no role for the siding in the electric era to come, it was removed in 1937.

Immediately West of the station island platform is Bidston Dee Junction where the ex-Great Central double track diverges to curve sharply Southwards to persue its way along the peninsula. The signal box controlling the junction is on the Up side and is a neat, conventionally-styled brick and timber structure built by the LMS in 1937 to replace the former Wirral Railway box here and also its neighbour at Bidston, West Junction, the one new box now performing all the work in the station area.

The view from Bidston station footbridge was once a grand vista of Bidston Hill with its wooded slopes to the South, fields and flat countryside to the West, golf links to the North and the skyline of Wallasey and the docks upon looking Eastwards, but since the late 1960's all has changed. The Wirral Motorway, opened in 1971 crossed the line immediately beyond Dee Junction, its bridge blocking the view Westwards and since that was completed, connecting roads and the Bidston by-pass have resulted in the once rural station achieving the perhaps unique distinction of being completely surrounded by motorways — North, South, East and West! Such, of course, is progress! Development of new housing estates nearby soon brought change, and the once neat, tidy station with its flower beds became dilapidated and defaced, its flowers and shrubs trampled under unappreciative feet.

Between Bidston and Leasowe the line still passes between fields but for how much longer? Already multi-storey flats dominate the skyline in nearby Upton, whilst housing developments continue to obliterate the countryside. In contrast Leasowe Castle is not far from the line — not a real castle but a large building, 300 years old, used for many years as a railway convalescent home. The tower of the long-disused Leasowe lighthouse can also be seen from the trains.

Leasowe station has a level crossing over Reeds Lane at its East end and a small signal box adjacent to it on the Down side of the line.

This signal box, a conventional-style timber one was built in 1937 to replace a former ground lever-frame. The station itself was rebuilt under the electrification scheme and is completely modern. Between Leasowe and Moreton is a built-up area, largely developed since the end of World War 2 on fields that were once covered in gorse and other vegetation, among which sparks from passing locomotives used to initiate some spectacular conflagrations during spells of hot and dry weather.

Moreton was once a village, and the seashore nearby attracted many visitors even before the vast post-war development. The place was marshy and subject to flooding in Winter — a bleak place indeed, that has changed out of all recognition in recent years and is now a small town with almost every amenity provided. Cadbury's biscuit factory opened in 1953 dominates the scene on the Up side of the line on the Leasowe side of Moreton station. The premises were originally rail-served, the sidings being laid amid pleasant lawns and flower beds. The headshunt track terminated in the factory sports ground, surrounded by neatly trimmed grass! Traffic was in vans, whilst fuel came in open 16 ton mineral wagons and these vehicles were shunted by a small diesel locomotive that was decked out in a livery somewhat resembling a chocolate bar wrapper. Trains for the factory arrived mainly by the Great Central line, reversing direction at Bidston, outgoing trains performing the operation in reverse. A few trains used the Hooton-West Kirby line until its closure. Alas, all rail traffic at the factory ceased in about 1971 but the rails remained in place for several years afterwards. The site of the former sidings has now been covered by new buildings.

Moreton station was completely rebuilt for the electrification of course, the old corrugated iron and timber huts and cinder platforms being replaced by modern bricks and concrete. A small goods and coal yard was formerly situated on the South side of the line at the East end of the passenger station, but this was closed in 1965 and the rails removed. A small signal box of conventional style replaced the old Wirral railway cabin in 1937. This has a pronounced "L&NWR" look and was probably built from spare materials from demolished signal boxes elsewhere. It is situated on the Up side of the line East of the station.

The main road crosses the railway on a stone arch bridge at the west end of Moreton station, beyond which is the Moreton Brick Works, an old-established manufactury that had a railway siding, which was removed in 1954 after a long period of disuse. The firm also had its own railway wagons until Nationalisation. Once the brick works and a few cottages were the only buildings in the vicinity of Moreton station, but the scene is vastly different nowadays.

Beyond Moreton, countryside still exists to a fair degree. The railway passes over Carr Lane level crossing, the gates being controlled by a ground frame housed in a small hut on the Down side of the line. Continuing through a landscape of fields, gorse, and marshland, the railway next approaches Meols, a former village and small seaside resort now very greatly developed. Behind the South platform of the modernised station lies the large expanse of the Meols Pond. This feature, legend has it, was created by Braithwaite Poole to lure anglers in Summer and ice skaters in Winter, who would travel on the trains to reach it and thus provide some extra revenue for the railway! The road to Saughall Massie passes over the railway by a bridge at the West end of the station. Being a purely passenger station, there were no sidings at Meols.

Proceeding onwards the railway curves gradually South-Westwards. Recent developments have spread housing estates over the area. Some of this activity began during the 1930's and it was for this reason that the LMS Company had a new station built at Manor Road in 1938, which in the style of the period is constructed in bricks and concrete. The station was not completed until after the commencement of electric train services and consequently no steam train ever called there with the exception of the New Brighton-London service, which continued to be a steam train after electrification.

Hoylake is the station following Manor Road. Before the railway came this place was a fishing village and small resort, which also had a race course. It developed as a genteel "watering place" and residential area during late Victorian times and has expanded quite considerably in more recent years. The station is well situated on the main road (Station Road), which continues as Carr Lane on the opposite side of the level crossing which is at the West end of the platforms. The signal box, one of the few remaining of Wirral railway origin is on the Up side of the line adjacent to the crossing.

Hoylake had quite a large amount of track until recent times. On the North side of the line, East of the platforms there were two long carriage sidings which were used for holding electric trains, but they were removed about 1978. On the South side there is still a long siding that sees regular use, whilst there were formerly spur lines to the Hoylake gas works and to the former Wirral Railway Company's carriage works and paint shop. Although the latter were closed by the LMS Company during the 1920's, the buildings and associated sidings were left in position. In addition to these lines, there were goods and coal sidings. The latter were closed in 1965, whilst the gas works ceased to receive coal by rail. Shortly afterwards all the track was removed and the site of the goods yard and old workshops is now occupied by industrial buildings. All that remains today is the aforementioned carriage siding. The rails serving the former work-shops are believed to have been among the last "Wirral" track to exist, all the main lines and many sidings having been re-laid since 1923, a lot of ex-L&NWR material being used to refurbish sidings.

29

The "open" character of the scenery begins to alter beyond Hoylake, more so on the West side of the line where development of the village took place in Victorian times when large, red-brick villas were built and golf links established. There are still fields on the East side of the railway however, until the environs of West Kirby are approached, when buildings nestle close to the line on both sides. Bridge Road passes over the line, appropriately via a bridge and on the South side of this structure the junction with the former branch to Hooton was situated, controlled by a conventional-style brick and timber signal box on the Up side, this having been built in 1937 to replace the former all-timber Wirral Railway box here. The terminus of the main Wirral line is more or less straight ahead, the island platform station being flanked by sidings and a coal yard on the Down side. The coal yard was closed in November, 1965 however, and since then much track removal has taken place in the vicinity of the station including one carriage siding. The Hooton Branch curved to the left, to become single track after passing through West Kirby "Joint" station. Further curved sidings flanked this line in the station area. Here, in pre-Grouping days the Wirral trains with their black engines and brown carriages met with the green engines and chocolate-and-cream carriages of the Great Western Railway, also the black engines and purple-brown and white vehicles of the L&NWR. After the Grouping it was black engines and red coaches of the LMS but the Great Western colours remained as before.

West Kirby station consists of a wide island platform, with a concrete canopy that was installed in 1937. The station buildings, of red brick and quite pleasing in design are clustered in Grange Road and are enhanced by a clock tower. The station is at street level and conveniently situated for local residents, whilst being only a few minutes walk from the shore for visitors who come by train. Grange Road climbs steeply to cross the former Hooton Branch track and passes Caldy Hill with its well-known column at the summit. West Kirby station preserves its Victorian looks by virtue of its red-brick buildings. Old Wirral Railway signs and notices lingered for many years after Nationalisation. One of these bore the words "Parcels and Cloaks" — a real "period-piece" that duly received the red and cream paint of British Railways! Standard enamelled metal signs have since replaced these survivors from other years.

Water columns for the steam locomotives were provided at Birkenhead Park and West Kirby, located,at the outer ends of the platforms. The ritual of filling up was often watched by small boys who stood very close, and had to leap away quickly to dodge the cascade of water that splashed around when the fireman, up on the engine tank, slung the "bag" out of the engine's tank-filler hole. During frosty weather coke braziers were lit to prevent the water freezing, their warm glow adding some measure of cheeriness to an otherwise bleak scene.

Returning now to Bidston East Junction, the New Brighton line next claims attention. This swings away from the main line, curving to the right at the latter junction and presently joins the curve from Bidston West Junction at Seacombe Junction, the signal box here being a conventional-style brick and timber edifice of LMS design which replaced a former all-timber Wirral signal box in 1937. The box controls not only the junction of the lines from Birkenhead and Bidston, but as its name implies, the junction at which the New Brighton and former Seacombe lines diverged. Between Birkenhead North and Seacombe Junction the railway, with several long curved sidings on the Up side passes along a low embankment near the Western extremity of Birkenhead Docks. From a distance ocean-going ships give the impression of being stranded in the fields in this area! To the right is a vista of cranes, sheds, huge tanks for the storage of molasses or oil, chimneys and ships, whilst to the left the flat landscape of this part of Wirral stretches away, reminding one of Holland. The wooded slopes of Bidston Hill overlook the scene from the South. Following World War 2 a new berth for handling iron ore was built at Bidston Dock and was provided with a double track rail connection from Seacombe Junction. This brought new and regular traffic direct from the dock to the great and extensive John Summers steel works at Shotton, until this establishment closed in the late 1970's. The heavy ore trains, hauled by the largest steam locomotives ever to run on former Wirral Railway tracks — the class 9F 2-10-0's, later by diesel locomotives, travelled via the former Great Central line, leaving the Wirral line at Bidston, Dee Junction.

Still on a low embankment, the New Brighton line curves North-Westerly at Seacombe Junction passing fields and golf courses on the left, whilst the buildings of Liscard and Poulton lay some little distance away on the right. The derelict and overgrown course of the connecting line that once made the direct New Brighton-Seacombe service possible is visible on the right as the track curves towards Wallasey village, passing allotments and recent housing developments. The new motorways now dominate this scene, of course.

Wallasey Village station was opened in 1907 under the name of Leasowe Road, to serve the spreading residential area, which has expanded even more in the years since the end of the war in 1945. The line crosses Leasowe Road by the only rail-over-road bridge on the former Wirral system and more recently, widening of this busy road has necessitated the provision of a new bridge of considerable dimensions spanning the now dual carriageway. In 1969 the new motorway linking with the second Mersey tunnel was carried across the line near the site of the former triangular junction and the character of the area has been considerably altered. No sidings or facilities for goods traffic have ever been provided at Wallasey Village station — it has always been a purely passenger facility. The title "village" is a misnomer nowadays!

31

Only a quarter of a mile or so beyond Wallasey Village station is that of Wallasey, Grove Road, a much grander one than any other intermediate station on the system, being built in red brick work and quite commodious, with a spacious forecourt and approach road. Goods and coal traffic facilities were provided in a large yard beyond the station on the North side of the line, a loop line (which was electrified but was hardly ever used for electric trains) and two sidings together with a goods shed being available. The goods traffic facilites were withdrawn in November 1965 however, the loop and sidings thereafter being removed and the goods shed demolished. The signal box, an all timber one of Wirral Railway origin was on the Down side of the line opposite the goods shed, and was done away with when the goods traffic (latterly only domestic coal) ceased.

The railway passes beneath Harrison Drive a short distance beyond Grove Road station, and next curves North-Eastwards, running parallel to the coast in a sandy area, with Harrison Park and golf links on the South side of the line. The long.vanished Warren station, which served the golf links in pre-motoring days was situated on this stretch of line just beyond Sea Road bridge (now demolished). The scene changes as New Brighton is approached, the line entering a pleasant tree-shaded cutting, after which it runs into the terminal station.

The section between Wallasey and New Brighton includes the only gradients of any consequence on the Wirral line, with inclinations of 1 in 88 to 1 in 100, and presented the small locomotives of old with a difficult task in the Summer months, during which they hauled heavy, crowded trains full of day trippers bound for the seaside.

When the Wallasey embankment and promenade were being extended during the 1930's sidings were provided near New Brighton so that material for the constructional works could be brought by rail. The contractor had a green Saddle tank locomotive which was a familiar sight among the sandhills until the work was completed in 1939, after which the temporary tracks were removed.

New Brighton station, on steeply inclined Atherton Street, is only a short distance from the promenade. It consists of an island platform, with all the buildings at the roadway end. Like West Kirby station, it is in red brick and features a clock tower. A run-round loop is provided either side of the island platform, whilst two long sidings come between the passenger station and adjacent goods shed, behind which a goods and coal yard with several sidings was situated. This was closed in November 1965 however. Portland Street crosses the line by an overbridge at the outer end of the station, whilst on the South side of the station a wooded slope lies adjacent to Victoria Road with its elegant and elderly houses overlooking the railway. The signal box, of all-timber Wirral Railway design is on the Down side West of Portland Street bridge, under which the headshunt of the goods sidings passed alongside the main lines. Here too in earlier years a spur line ran to the shore of the Mersey estuary and was probably used for sand traffic. It was removed sometime in the early LMS period, but its former course can still be traced.

For many years excursion trains have been run to New Brighton during the Spring and Summer seasons, bringing types of locomotives not normally seen in the Wirral district. Many of these trains came from the Midlands and Yorkshire, worked throughout by Great Central locomotives, later L&NER types, and such trains continued to be operated for many years into the British Railways era, latterly with diesel-electric locomotives and DMU sets. Excursion traffic has fallen off in recent times however and New Brighton is no longer the resort it was, though car ownership has been the main reason for the decline in the popularity of excursion traffic, even those who made the trip over by train from Liverpool on Sundays and Bank Holidays no longer do so in the enormous numbers that called for many extra trains and additional station staff in the years before, and for some time after, World War 2.

Having surveyed the New Brighton line we must now return to Seacombe Junction and go back a few years to examine, in past tense, the now vanished Seacombe Branch. This persued a sinuous course in a generally Easterly direction after leaving Seacombe Junction, to pass through rock cuttings and beneath numerous street overbridges to reach its terminal near Seacombe ferry stage. Shortly before the line passed under Breck Road bridge, the connection with the lines on Birkenhead Dock estate, the single track Slopes Branch, diverged on the Up side at Slopes Branch signal box (ex-Wirral), this also being situated on the Up side of the line. The Slopes Branch, which was opened in 1907, persued its course between fences and hedges for some distance, then emerged from its reservation to cross Poulton Bridge Road via a level crossing, the gates being opened and closed by the train men. The branch continued onwards unfenced alongside the roadway to join up with the extensive system of dockside lines. The branch probably acquired its title from that of a large residence in Breck Road called "The Slopes". For a time this was the home of Mr. Newell of the contractors Monk & Newell. The once busy Slopes Branch fell gradually into eventual disuse during the 1950's and traffic on it ceased altogether in 1959. After lying derelict and overgrown for some months, the rails were removed.

The only intermediate station on the Seacombe Branch was that of Licard & Poulton, located on Mill Lane. It was an island platform with simple timber buildings and, being situated in a cutting, was reached by stairs from the road overbridge. Between Breck Road bridge and the station, a spur line diverged from the Up line and served a quarry, which was closed long ago.

Beyond Liscard station the Wallasey gas and electricity works were situated on the South side of the railway, their grounds covered by many sidings holding lines of wagons laden with coal. A single-line spur gave access to the works from the Wirral line, whilst they were also accessible from the dock lines. Gas holders, chimneys and buildings dominated the scene here for many years until post-war changes caused the works to cease using rail, and during the early 1960's all the sidings and the main line connection were removed. Most of the works buildings have now gone too.

Further along the Seacombe Branch, Gorsey Lane crossed the line by a bridge and a little distance beyond, Seacombe Goods signal box was located, and a group of sidings on the Down side ran parallel with Gorsedale Road. These were referred to as Egremont Sidings — sometimes as Oakdale Road Sidings. On the Up side of the railway an industrial skyline indicated the closeness of the Wallasey and Birkenhead Docks.

One of the last uses of Egremont Sidings was for the storage of a large number of new 21-ton steel hopper wagons, which for some reason could not be put into service and they stood idle here for nearly two years! There were more of them parked at Bidston. The sidings remained in situ until the branch was closed. Continuing onwards the railway passed under several road bridges and after the final one — Church Street, emerged from the cutting and entered an open area at Victoria Place, only a short distance from the Mersey ferry landing stage.

Seacombe station, entitled Seacombe & Egremont (the latter being a district about a mile or so down the river) consisted of a single platform on the South side and an island platform. Between the side and island platforms were two tracks forming a run-round loop, two tracks also forming a loop being situated on the Down side of the island. Opposite the station on its North side there was a goods yard, which was closed and the sidings removed before the passenger service ceased, of which more later. The station was a primitive one, consisting of a collection of corrugated iron and timber shacks and few improvements were ever made except for the rebuilding of the island platform with concrete facings after Nationalisation and the installation of electric lighting in place of gas at a more recent date, both improvements having a short life as events turned out. After the Seacome-West Kirby LMS train service was withdrawn in March, 1938, the single platform saw very little use, but remained in situ until the end.

Seacombe signal box was situated on the Down side of the line on the Poulton side of Church Road bridge. An ex-Wirral Railway structure, it bore a large nameboard on the front which read "Seacombe Station Cabin". Until the end a large ex-L&NWR bracket post with three arms and two subsidiary signals governed the station entrance. Apart from a daily goods and coal train the only shunting movements were engines running round their trains ready for departure. Prior to March, 1938 the station was used by LMS trains on the West Kirby service and LNER trains to Wrexham, also excursions, and was a busy place, especially during the Summer when large numbers of day trippers used the trains.

Only a few-hundred yards from Seacombe station, an extremity of the docks railway, laid alongside the public street, served coal yards situated along Birkenhead Road and East Street near the ferry stage, but no connection was ever made between the dock lines and the passenger station of Seacombe.

There remains the section of railway between Birkenhead Park station and Bidston East Junction to be looked at before passing on to other facets of the Wirral Railway scene. At "Park" (it was always thus abreviated) the Wirral system met the metals of the Mersey Railway end-on at the fairly commodious station situated in an earthen cutting. Until changes made in the early 1970's, Park station consisted of two wide island platforms, both liberally provided with canopies supported on iron columns in the best Victorian railway style. Four main tracks passed through the station, two being used by the Mersey Railway and two by the Wirral Company, with sidings on either side of the station. The modern LMS-style signal box on the South platform replaced a former Mersey Railway flat-roofed box in 1937. On the Down side of the station, there existed until recently several long sidings which were used mainly by the engineering department for unloading stores and materials including rails and sleepers etc. Normal goods traffic was not dealt with, at least in more recent times. The Mersey Railway had its own stabling sidings and car shed on the North side of the main lines here, but the latter was destroyed by bombs in 1941. The usual vehicles to be seen at "Park" were bogie bolster wagons, low and high sided open wagons and occasionally goods vans, also brake vans and various converted passenger coaches demoted to departmental duties.

Birkenhead Park was, for much of its life, an interchange station, the through running between Mersey and Wirral systems having lasted only for a few years and there were no through services again until 1938. In the old days, Mersey Railway locomotives, which spent their working days beneath the ground in perpetual darkness met with those of the Wirral system which travelled through the fair green countryside and alongside the sea. Often must Mersey drivers and firemen have envied their Wirral colleagues, especially on golden Summer days, when instead of driving through a long, dark tunnel, travelled through the fields to West Kirby or enjoyed the bracing breezes of the New Brighton line!

Proceeding Westwards from Birkenhead Park the Wirral line describes an elongated 'S', passing through a short tunnel beneath Brassey Street and Cavendish Street and traverses an earthen cutting

35

which is spanned by several road overbridges in a residential area. This cutting extends as far as Birkenhead North station which is situated on Station Road that leads to Stanley Road, the latter thoroughfare passing above the railway at the West end of the station, continuing to become Wallasey Bridge Road on which the original Hoylake Railway station existed long ago. Birkenhead North has a single platform on the Down side and also an island platform, with a loop and siding on the North side of the station. Birkenhead North No.1 signal box (ex-Wirral Railway) occupies a position at the West end of the Down platform. During 1937 an electrical control room and sub-station was built at the East end and interested passengers can sometimes catch a glimpse of the wierd blue glow from the mercury-arc rectifiers as their train passes, if they look carefully.

The aforementioned siding was originally longer than it is today and rose to a higher level than the main lines. It was reduced to its present length in 1966. The loop line has an extension at the West end which joins the extensive sidings of the train sheds and maintenance depot West of Station Road.

Upon leaving North station the line curves North-Westwards, then swings West again and the land suddenly becomes almost flat. To the right lay the old Wirral Railway locomotive depot, carriage sheds and sidings, with an industrial and dockland background, and since 1938 the large electric car sheds. On the left-hand side Bidston Hill rises upwards in the background, whilst nearer at hand was the former Great Central Railway Bidston locomotive depot (closed in 1963). A large group of marshalling sidings parallelled the main line on the Down side, whilst a double track branch, laid in 1907 emerged from the marshalling yard and made connection with the railway system of Birkenhead Docks. The branch crossed the River Birket (a narrow stream) on a timber tressle bridge, which was replaced by a concrete bridge in 1957, and next crossed the Wirral main line by a set of diamond crossings. By 1969 the once busy sidings had become largely disused and were sometimes almost devoid of rolling stock in contrast to the hundreds of wagons that could be seen here only a few years previously. All tracks of the former Great Central at Bidston were removed in 1972, leaving a barren wasteland where once had been ceaseless activity. A large steel works, not rail served, has recently been built on the site.

Adjacent to the previously mentioned GC branch crossing of the main line, is Birkenhead North No.2 signal box, new in 1937 and of conventional-style, which replaced a former Wirral Railway box. It stands on the Down side of the line. Tracks leading to the electric car sheds and various sidings spread out on the right, whilst several long sidings laid on made-up ground and very over-grown run Westwards onto Bidston Moss. Looking to the left again, an expanse of cinders marks the site of a small carriage shed which was destroyed in the "blitz" of 1940. It had been little used since electrification however, and the rails were removed from the site in 1941.

Bidston East Junction signal box is next reached, this being on the Down side and is another LMS structure of conventional-style that replaced an old Wirral box here. The line taken by trains to New Brighton diverges to the right, to join the line from Bidston West Junction at Seacombe Junction. Bidston West Junction, which had its own signal box until 1938, is now controlled from Bidston Dee Junction signal box. The narrow River Birket passes beneath the railway in a long tunnel near Bidston West Junction. This river, which originates at West Kirby follows the railway over most of its length between the latter place and Birkenhead.

The only locomotive depot on the Wirral Railway was situated at Birkenhead North. It was largely a locomotive "yard", because the shed was an inadequate structure that resembled a farmyard outbuilding rather than a railway facility, and consequently the locomotives spent a large proportion of their lives out in the open air. Sheer-legs were provided so that engines could be lifted for wheel removal, as quite heavy repairs were carried out there in pre-Grouping days. The Wirral Railway possessed no such luxury as a locomotive works. Major overhauls were carried out at Gorton, Manchester, by Beyer, Peacock and Company, makers of most of the company's locomotives, whilst lesser tasks beyond the scope of Birkenhead North depot were dealt with at the Mersey Railway works at Birkenhead Central until that company electrified its lines. In LMS days after the 1923 Grouping, Wirral section locomotives went to Crewe, Horwich or Derby for overhaul.

A prominent feature of Birkenhead North locomotive depot was its curious water tank which resembled a zeppelin mounted on a brickwork plinth! Although the depot closed in 1938, this tank was still in situ in 1969. It appears in many photographs of Wirral engines taken over the years. After closure, locomotives on goods and trip workings still took water at the old tank but steam has been gone from the Wirral for a long time now.

Passenger and goods rolling stock was overhauled in a small works near the North locomotive depot, an old stables dating from tramway days forming part of this establishment that was too small to carry out the full range of work, hence the "outpost" at Hoylake mentioned earlier. The LMS company closed these small workshops.

The Wirral, being purely a "tank engine" railway had little need for turntables, but one existed at Birkenhead North for many years. This was removed by the LMS company in 1925, and if for any reason a locomotive needed turning, the maneouvre could be carried out by running it round the Bidston "triangle".

The frequent train service called for reliable and smart work on the

37

part of both locomotives and men, and the shortness of the journeys meant that uncoupling and running round trains and re-coupling had to be carried out numerous times in the course of a day's work. These operations were performed at a remarkable speed and, at a terminal station, by the time alighting passengers were streaming past what had been the front of the train, the engine would already have been detached and run forward beyond the crossover, ready to run round the train and be coupled up again ready for another journey. As soon as the train arrived at the platform, the fireman would alight from the engine just as the wheels had ceased to turn, then drop down between it and the first coach and uncouple them, where upon the engine was driven forward towards the buffer-stops. This was followed by the fireman proceeding to the adjacent lever-frame and pulling over the points, re-setting them after the engine had reversed and cleared them, after which he swung aboard to ride to the other end of the train to re-couple, the crossover points at the outer end of the station being set by the signalman. The speed with which these operations were carried out equalled, if it did not actually surpass the quick turn-round of today's multiple-unit diesel train sets.

The locomotives were worked extremely hard, and at holiday times most of the fleet at Birkenhead North depot would be in traffic, slogging to and fro with capacity train-loads. In order to reduce line occupation to a minimum at extra-busy times (usually Summer Sundays), it was the practice to send engines that had finished their turns back to the depot on the front of a passenger train, so that a train might have two or even three engines at the head end. This practice evoked much comment and query on the part of passengers, some with little knowledge of railway operation, being led into the belief that things must have been in a bad way if a six-coach train needed three engines to haul it! The expressions of stupefied amazement on the faces of motorists held up at the level crossings was worth seeing on such occasions, whilst the sound effects produced from the engines as the train got moving from each station was such as to enrapture any locomotive devotee, who certainly received plenty of interest and entertainment in return for his modest fare! At Birkenhead North the homegoing engine, or engines, were removed from the train and proceeded to the shed, the train being halted some distance outside the station to enable this to be done. The enginemen seemed to enjoy these occasions, revelling in observing the expressions on the faces of onlookers and passengers.

A once busy interchange station, the much altered Birkenhead Park complex presents a scene of total desertion in this May 1983 view. The left-hand platform with original canopy is disused, whilst the widened "Down" platform covers a former track used by the Mersey Railway. The signal box is of LM&S design, built in 1937. (Photo: S.G. Jones).

A train for Liverpool arriving at Birkenhead North station, May 1983. (Photo: S.G. Jones).

The vastly developed Wallasey Village is the only place on the Wirral line where trains cross above a road. In earlier times the Railway passed over a country lane by a level crossing at this location. Photograph shows 1983 scene. (Photo: S.G. Jones).

Wallasey (Grove Road), one of the better stations on the old Wirral Railway has changed little over the years. A train for Birkenhead is entering the station, hauled by a 0-4-4 Tank locomotive. (Photo: J. Ryan collection).

The pleasant, tree-shaded cutting at the approach to New Brighton station, May 1983. In Wirral Railway days a spur line passed through the gate and led to the seashore. In this area sand had to be constantly removed to prevent the track being buried, but this has not been necessary since the dunes were levelled and starr grass planted. (Photo: S.G. Jones).

The signal box at New Brighton station is situated in picturesque surroundings. This is one of the few ex-Wirral railway signal boxes that survived into the 1980's. May, 1983. (Photo: S.G. Jones).

New Brighton station in Wirral Railway days. The small lever frame for working the points of the engine run-round loop is visible in the lower left-hand corner. One of Wallasey's "sea green" trams passes along the adjacent road. (Photo: J. Ryan collection).

New Brighton station in May, 1983. A Liverpool bound train stands at the platform whilst spare trains in the sidings await the peak traffic hours. The new building on the left occupies the site of the former goods and coal sidings. (Photo: S.G. Jones).

The Rolling Stock

The history of the Wirral Railway company's passenger carriages and goods vehicles differs but little from that of most other small local railways. At the opening of the Hoylake Railway in 1866 small four-wheeled carriages with half-open compartments and wooden seats in the Second and Third classes were the order of the day. These vehicles were second-hand and subsequent early additions were similar, although six-wheeled carriages appeared in due course. Even as late as 1903 the fleet of four-wheeled carriages was increased by the purchase of a number of former Mersey Railway vehicles made redundant by electrification. These were instantly recognisable by the half-round door vents, a feature found also on carriages of the London Metropolitan and Great Eastern systems. Some four-wheeled carriages were also obtained from the Midland Railway company. Early carriages were lit by oil lamps, a form of illumination which was later replaced by gas.

In 1888 four new set trains were obtained, the vehicles being gas-lit and in 1896 several eight-wheeled bogie carriages with eliptical roofs were supplied by the Birmingham Railway Carriage & Wagon Company. There were no more additions until 1910, when further bogie vehicles were introduced, composed of new underframes and bogies, on each of which was mounted the bodies of two old four-wheeled carriages which, with a general refurbishing resulted in quite comfortable and presentable vehicles although their low curved roofs gave them an old-fashioned appearance. The conversion work was carried out in the small workshop at Hoylake.

A typical set-train on the Wirral lines in pre-Grouping days consisted of a mixture of six-wheeled and bogie carriages with a six-wheeled brake and luggage van either end. The livery of the passenger vehicles was chocolate, with the ends of brake carriages and brake vans painted red, a rare custom practised also by the London, Brighton & South Coast and Highland Railways. The idea seems to have been to make the ends of trains conspicious, but the practice was not followed by the four main line companies after the Grouping.

During a period of shortage due to many vehicles being laid up for repairs after the 1914-1918 war, a number of passenger carriages were hired from the London & North Western and Great Central Railways, and it is believed that some were purchased from both these companies.

After the Grouping of 1923 further six-wheeled carriages from the L&NW and L&Y Railways were drafted to the Wirral lines along with several sets of bogie vehicles (vintage 1890's) of L&NWR origin with low-curved roofs. Some L&Y bogie carriages also arrived and the bogie vehicles, along with a few LMS-built vehicles maintained the services until electrification. Each rake of coaches carried a board on either end which read "Wirral Section Set Number —". All the draftees were in their original colours at first but gradually the "Midland Red" of the LMS eliminated the old pre-1923 liveries, although some years elapsed before the task of repainting was completed.

Shortly after the amalgamations the Wirral carriages began to vanish and in a brief period of time the appearance of the trains had altered completely. The stock at the time of Grouping consisted of 71 carriages and one mail van. This latter vehicle was sold to a former railwayman who used it as a dwelling at Moreton where, still on its wheels, it survived until about 1953. The bodies of one or two other Wirral carriages were used as sheds and hutments and one was still in situ adjacent to Slopes Branch signal cabin as late as 1960. At the time of electrification there were 70 coaches in use on the Wirral lines, all being bogie vehicles of mixed ancestry, with building dates ranging from 1893 to 1932 and all were of non-corridor compartment type. The regular formations were four-coach sets but a number of two-coach sets were kept for strengthening purposes at busy times.

The Wirral Railway being predominantly a passenger carrying system had only a small fleet of goods vehicles — about one hundred all told. About 50 of them were open merchandise wagons. There were 15 wagons for locomotive coal and a mere three goods vans. One gas holder truck and 14 goods brake vans made up the remainder of the fleet. The last-named vehicles were mainly used on trains of rolling stock from other railways working to and from Birkenhead Docks. Coal traffic, domestic and industrial was chiefly carried in privately owned wagons belonging to merchants and collieries. In British Railways days, coal traffic, where it remained was handled in the ubiquitous steel 16-ton mineral wagons which replaced the former P.O. fleets and became familiar over the whole of Britain's railway system. More recently coal for domestic use is brought to the concentration depot at Birkenhead North in B.R. steel hopper wagons.

The marshy expanse of Bidston Moss forms the background to this view of a train of vintage Great Central rolling stock, including six-wheeled carriages, hauled by an ex-GC 4-4-2 Tank engine of Class C.13. The train is probably an excursion from Seacombe to Caergwrle Castle in North Wales, many of which were run in L&NER days and were very popular. (Photo: J. Ward collection).

A West Kirby to Birkenhead Park train approaching Birkenhead North in June, 1936, hauled by 2-6-2 Tank engine No.42. The four-coach set train of vintage L&NWR coaches has been strengthened by the addition of two extra vehicles, also ex-L&NWR but of more recent design. (Photograph: W. Potter).

LM&SR 0-4-4 Tank engine No.6406 on a West Kirby – Birkenhead Park train passing over the Great Central crossing at Bidston East Junction on 3rd October, 1937. The third-rail for electrification is in position. (Photo: F. Hewitt).

Hoylake station signal box – a survivor from the Wirral Railway era, still in use in 1983. (Photo: S.G. Jones).

The New Electric Era

As far back as the year 1900 proposals were made to electrify the Wirral Railway and funds were set aside for such a project, but the amount was not sufficient and the task was not put in hand by the company. It was not until 1936, deep into LMS days, that a final decision was taken to change from steam to electric operation.

The work of electrifying the Wirral lines commenced in 1936. This involved largely relaying the track, laying the conductor rail, building sub-stations, and ancilliary works. Reconstruction of stations was also involved, the former primitive structures at Bidston, Leasowe, Moreton, Meols, Hoylake and Wallasey Village being transformed by reinforced concrete and glass, whilst the open platforms of West Kirby and New Brighton received concrete canopies. All station platforms were increased in height, flagged, paved and given concrete facings. Electric lighting replaced oil and gas lamps. Another major task was the construction of the large Car shed and Workshop nearby the steam locomotive depot at Birkenhead North.

Certain track alterations were carried out at Bidston chiefly involving re-modelling of the West junction, the Seacombe line now diverging close-by the station and running parallel with the Birkenhead line for a short distance before curving away, instead of the former arrangement were it directly left the main line some distance from the station. The re-siting of the junction brought about the demolition of the signal cabin, the points now being worked from Dee Junction box. The sidings and GC reception lines on the Down side remained, and so did the level crossings, but the refuge siding on the Up side of the passenger station, long disused, was removed. A plate-girder bridge, of single track width, probably intended for some development that never materialised was removed during the alterations. This crossed the Birket just in front of the portal of the long culvert that takes the stream beneath the railway.

Signalling of the semaphore type was retained throughout the newly electrified lines, but many of the older lower-quadrant signals on timber posts were replaced by standard upper-quadrant signals on tubular steel posts. Even so, some former L&NWR signals installed earlier by the LMS to replace Wirral Railway signals survived for many years after electrification, notably the Up line gantry approaching Birkenhead Park at the tunnel portal, which was still in use in 1965. Somewhat remarkably, two Wirral lower-quadrant signals on lattice steel posts continued in use at Hoylake, these being the Up Starting and Down Home signals. They were still in use in 1973, but have now been replaced. The Hoylake Down Home signal, an L&NWR replacement for a Wirral signal was also still in use that year, and was actually repainted during April. Track-circuiting was installed throughout the system in order that the intensified train service could be safely and efficiently operated. In recent times semaphore signals have been gradually replaced by colour-lights on the section between Birkenhead Park and Bidston, though some semaphores were still in use in 1983.

The line between Seacombe Junction and Seacombe terminus was not included in the electrification scheme, LMS trains being withdrawn from it when the electric services commenced, and thus the character of this last Wirral Railway extension remained unchanged. It was the beginning of the end however, as events subsequently proved.

When the Wirral electrification commenced the power supply was taken from Clarence Dock Power Station, Liverpool, at that time owned by the Liverpool Corporation. Cables were laid through the Mersey Railway tunnel for the purpose. Today the current for the combined Wirral and Mersey lines comes from the Central Electricity Generating Board. The supply at 11kv, 3-phase, 50 cycles which, after being received at the main sub-station and control point at Birkenhead North, is distributed to a further five unmanned sub-stations throughout the system, each equipped with glass bulb type mercury-arc rectifiers which are rated at 600kw and convert the incoming A.C. supply to 650 volts D.C. for traction purposes. Elaborate safeguards and a communications system are maintained to deal with any emergency and to isolate sections of line if necessary.

New servicing facilites were of course, required for the electric trains, which were provided in the shape of the large shed and workshops on the Up side of the line at Birkenhead North mentioned earlier in the description of the line. The old carriage shed on the Up side, also mentioned earlier was retained for stabling electric rolling stock and when it was destroyed in the air raids in 1940, four vehicles inside it were damaged beyond repair, these being two trailer and two driving trailer cars. Incidentally, the new shed was also badly damaged in the blitz, but subsequently rebuilt.

Electrification was completed early in 1938, the third-rail having been laid throughout and all cabling installed. Indeed, the line was energised from time to time and this meant that all employees had to take care where they walked and had to break the habit of stepping on rails when crossing the track. Trial trips with the electric trains were carried out from 3rd January, including the Mersey tunnel section, also for the purpose of training steam locomotive drivers as motormen.

The full electric train service commenced on Sunday, 13th March, 1938 with no ceremony and little fanfare. The official opening took place next day, of which more later. The need for passengers to change trains at Birkenhead Park was abolished, as the LMS trains were extended to Liverpool Central over the Mersey Railway, whilst trains of the latter company began working through to New Brighton, looking somewhat strange as they glided sedately through the fields and sandhills, the big clerestory-roofed cars with their end platforms being city-type rapid transit vehicles in every respect, though they got plenty of people to carry to and from their new destinations.

Goods traffic did not figure in the electrification scheme and was left to steam locomotive haulage. Never really heavy on this predominently passenger system, except on the Seacombe Branch, such goods traffic as there was tended to be of a local nature. Much of it was domestic coal for the towns and villages along the three lines, and a much heavier coal traffic for the Wallasey and Hoylake gas works, also the Wallasey electricity works. There was some longer-distance general goods traffic to and from Birkenhead and Wallasey docks via the Slopes Branch and Wirral line, but most of the really long-distance traffic went via Birkenhead (along Beaufort Road) or via the Great Central line which diverged from the Wirral system at Bidston. Some traffic was also exchanged with the L&NW/GW Joint line at West Kirby.

In earlier times the Wirral Railway relied on plenty of holiday traffic to keep the receipts on an even keel and a wet summer could prove serious for them as it could also for amusement caterers, restaurant proprietors and of course, the Wallasey ferries. Hot sunny days saw the trains packed to capacity, with people standing in the compartments and few seemed to mind such discomfort because it was of short-duration. The longest journey possible in a Wirral train lasted 40 minutes or so. Indeed, the system was so compact that vantage points existed from which one could follow the journeys of every train simply by watching the exhaust steam and smoke on the horizons, although on the Seacombe Branch the trains were lost to distant sight when traversing the cuttings beyond Poulton.

The Wirral lines continued to operate much as usual throughout the 1939-45 war except for increased traffic and difficulties caused by the black-out, plus staff shortages, with many of the men's jobs being taken over by women, as happened elsewhere, of course. During the air raids of 1940-41 the Wirral lines, although in the thick of the action and partly in vunerable areas, sustained remarkably little damage. Destruction of the Birkenhead North carriage shed and damage to the workshops has already been mentioned, but there was also damage caused to Wallasey Village station at which a bomb made a large crater on one of the platforms in May, 1941. Several bombs dropped around Bidston missed the railway, making craters in the surrounding fields. The line was straddled by some of the first bombs to fall on Merseyside, when in the early hours of Saturday, 10th August, 1940 several landed in Wallasey, on Adelaide Street and the side of the cutting on the Seacombe Branch which ran by the end of that thoroughfare. The Borough of Wallasey through which both the Seacombe and New Brighton lines passed received severe damage in raids between August 1940 and May 1941, but few incidents interupted train services to any great extent.

Extra passenger traffic was brought to the Wirral lines by the establishment of an army camp at Bidston in 1939, and an R.A.F. centre near West Kirby. Civilian traffic was also heavy as factories worked longer hours and employees worked in shifts, day and night. People also went in large numbers to New Brighton during the Summer months for a well-earned holiday or day trip in spite of increasing austerity conditions. Suspension of the popular Liverpool-New Brighton river ferry brought more traffic to the trains.

West Kirby station in 1937, showing the new canopy installed ready for the electric train services. A steam train consisting of elderly L&NWR rolling stock stands at the platform, whilst one of the new electric trains occupies the siding on the right. (LM&S Railway publicity photograph).

The cover of the first "electric" time table, March, 1938.

A Seacombe to Wrexham train hauled by ex-Great Central 0-6-2 T No.69274 arriving at Bidston station, on a Winter day in 1954. The concrete replacement of the former lengthy wooden footbridge is visible in the background. (Photo: G. Rose).

Seacombe station in its last decrepit days, with a train for Wrexham ready for departure. The engine is former Great Central 0-6-2 Tank No.69329 of Class N.5. built in 1899. This view was taken c.1955. (Photo: G. Rose).

Seacombe Branch Farewell

Before dealing with other aspects of the Wirral lines the subsequent history of the Seacombe Branch remains to be recorded. After electrification of the West Kirby and New Brighton lines, the Seacombe passenger service was abandoned by the LMS company and left to the L&NER, who continued to exercise their Running Powers between Bidston and Seacombe and operate their passenger train service to and from Wrexham, a somewhat unusual arrangement of one company running a complete service over tracks of another. The branch assumed an air of quietness and little importance in contrast to the quickened tempo of the other lines.

The Seacombe Branch lingered through the 1939-45 war under L&NER operation of the passenger trains that remained, and LMS/L&NER operation of goods traffic, and it survived for a little more than a decade under British Railways management. It saw no improvements whatever so far as the train services were concerned, and so became a candidate for closure when the blitz on branch lines got under way. By 1959 the service consisted of only 13 trains in each direction on weekdays and three each way on Sundays, so naturally, this sparse service did not encourage patronage. Moreover, passengers travelling from Liverpool to Wrexham or intermediate stations beyond Bidston were inclined to travel by the Mersey line and change at the latter place rather than taking the ferry from Liverpool Landing Stage and walking to Seacombe station even though the distance was only a matter of a couple of hundred yards.

During the late 1950's the goods and coal traffic was discontinued, Seacombe sidings were removed and the overgrown site became a demoralising portent of what was sure to follow with the passenger service. Patronage had declined to such an extent that when the proposal to close the branch completely was made in 1959, there was only a small amount of opposition. This proposed closure was a somewhat unusual case because the train service was actually being transferred to another line and instead of running between Bidston and Seacombe, was to run instead between Bidston and New Brighton.

The Seacombe Branch passenger train service finished in mid-Winter, on the night of Sunday, 3rd January, 1960. About 200 people braved the cold and ventured out into the darkness to witness the final departure, the 9.01 p.m. train to Wrexham, which left with ex-LMS 2-6-2 Tank locomotive No.41201 at the head, exploding fog signal detonators as it departed into the night. When this train had gone the crowd awaited the arrival of the last one from Wrexham, which drew in at 10.20 p.m. When this train had departed for Bidston with the empty coaches, the signalman locked up his box and the station staff locked the office, and business had finally ceased on the Seacombe Branch so far as passenger traffic was concerned.

On the following morning New Brighton station became busier, with an extra service of 14 trains on weekdays and six on Sundays, serving either Wrexham or Chester. The service was now provided by diesel train sets instead of steam, but was not much improvement over the previous one so far as the number of daily trains was concerned. Being able to reach Chester directly was an improvement however, though this facility was ultimately abandoned. Many people wondered why the diesel trains were not introduced on the Seacombe line, as New Brighton was not the ideal terminus for this particular service. In later years it was diverted to Birkenhead North which was much more satisfactory, but it has since been curtailed at Bidston.

Some goods traffic continued to use the Seacombe Branch between Bidston and Oakdale Road Sidings, part of the latter being used for wagon storage, but the final end came on 17th June 1963, when the branch was closed completely. Since that date the course of the line has slowly disappeared. The site of Seacombe station is now occupied by flats, whilst the cutting has been widened for a stretch to become an approach road for the second Mersey road tunnel. There is no rail traffic to the Wallasey gas and electricity works and no connection with the docks from the Wirral line remains except at Birkenhead North, via the level crossing over Wallasey Bridge Road, the Slopes Branch at Poulton having gone also, as mentioned previously.

A general view of the old Wirral engine shed at Birkenhead North in October 1937. LM&SR 0-6-0 "Standard Shunter" No.7353 is in the foreground. (Photo: F. Hewitt).

Ex-L&NWR 0-6-2 "Coal Tank" No.7711 at Birkenhead North, October 1937. Note the coal piled high in the bunker. (Photo: F. Hewitt).

The only former Wirral Railway engine to survive right through the LMS era and into British Railways days was the ex-Lancashire & Yorkshire 2-4-2 Tank, Wirral No.6 and later LMS 6762. Here it is at Preston as BR 46762 in early BR days. It was a familiar sight at Preston for many years, mainly employed on station pilot work. (Photo: J. Ward collection).

Resting at Birkenhead North on 3rd October, 1937 are 0-6-0 Tank No.7372, 2-6-2 Tank No.55, 0-6-2 "Coal Tanks" 27664 and 7780, plus unidentified 2-6-2 Tank. The low platform is the original Hoylake Railway station. (Photo: F. Hewitt).

The Vanished Engines

Tracing the early locomotive history of the Wirral Railway is difficult because detailed information is missing. When the Hoylake Railway was opened for traffic back in 1866 only two engines were on the company's strength. One is believed to have been a 2-2-2 Tank locomotive named "Ashton" which, after serving the company for about 15 years was sold to the Haydock Colliery near St. Helens. No information concerning the other locomotive appears to have survived. The two engines worked the sparse train service until the line was taken over by the Hoylake & Birkenhead Rail & Tramway Company in 1872 after which further motive power units were added.

In December, 1872, a 2-2-2 Well Tank locomotive named "Comet" was obtained. This engine with outside cylinders was built for service on the London & South Western Railway, at Nine Elms works, London in 1852. It worked on the Hoylake Railway until 1877 after which it was laid aside and was broken up for scrap in 1879. "Comet" had an entirely open footplate, so it was a cold, uncomfortable job for the enginemen in Winter, when the bitter sea winds swept across the bleak fields and marshes of Wirral, the small weatherboard on the engine giving little or no protection from the elements.

Another engine, apparently obtained about 1872, was a 2-4-0 Well Tank with inside cylinders, built by Sharp Stewart & Company in 1855, this too being devoid of any form of weather protection. This engine is believed to have started its working life on the North London Railway (to what diverse destinations North London engines migrated over the years!) But found its stay on the Hoylake line a short one indeed, for it was offered for sale again in 1874. As the engine was stated to be in good order, we can only conclude that it was too heavy for the track, or otherwise unsuitable for the company's operations. Its ultimate disposal is not known.

The year 1878 saw new locomotives ordered for the railway in the shape of two 2-4-0 Side Tanks with outside cylinders, both built by the Yorkshire Engine Company of Sheffield. They were numbered 1 and 2 and named "West Kirby" and "Birkenhead" respectively. These engines lasted until 1891, being then sold to concerns in Staffordshire. No.1 went to the Hardman Chemical Company at Milton. and No.2 to Talk o' the Hill Colliery.

In 1879 another second-hand engine arrived and this, believed to have been a 2-4-0 Saddle Tank with outside cylinders, came from the Neath & Brecon Railway in South Wales. It received the number 3 in the list of the Hoylake & Birkenhead Rail and Tramway Company and like its predecessors from other railways, had a short career in Wirral, being withdrawn for breaking-up in 1881.

In 1884 a new locomotive was ordered from Beyer, Peacock & Company of Manchester. This was a 2-4-0 Tank with inside cylinders which became number 3 of the Seacombe, Hoylake & Deeside Railway as the system was now entitled. It was followed by a similar engine from the same maker, which became No.4. Both engines had coupled wheels 5ft 0½in in diameter and cylinders measuring 15 x 20 inches. Their coal bunkers were of extremely small capacity, holding only 1½ tons but No.3 had coal rails fitted later, which increased the capacity to 2 tons. Both locomotives had a rather "Humpty-Dumpty" appearance that was accentuated by the deep water tanks and short bunkers. They spent much of their time on the Seacombe-New Brighton service and were withdrawn as follows: No.4 in January, 1913 and No.3 in February, 1914. Both ended up for scrap in the yard of Messrs. R. Smith & Son, Birkenhead, being disposed of together in February, 1914.

Five more new locomotives were added to stock in 1887-8, with a change of wheel arrangement this time, these engines being of the 0-4-4- Side Tank design, one which found much favour on railways with short-distance passenger traffic in the latter years of the nineteenth century. The engines, from Beyer, Peacock & Company, had cylinders measuring 16 x 24inches and coupled wheels 5ft 2inches in diameter. They became S.H&D Railway numbers 5, 6, 7, 8 and 9. Engine No.5 was renumbered 2 in 1894 and was in use until 1923. It was allocated the LMS number 6770 which was never carried as the scrap heap claimed it in that year of the railway Grouping.

Engine No.6 retained the same identity throughout its career and was withdrawn from regular service in June, 1921. It was retained for Departmental duties as No.6B for a few months more being finally withdrawn and broken up in January, 1922. Engine No.7 was renumbered 5 in 1894 and survived into LMS days although it never carried its allotted number 6771, being withdrawn in November, 1923. Engine No.8 retained the original number throughout its career, being allotted LMS number 6772 but never carried this due to the fact that it was withdrawn in October, 1923. No.9 lasted until April, 1924 but again, like its sisters, did not receive its allotted LMS number — 6773.

This batch of locomotives were quite neat in design though somewhat top-heavy looking and their rail-less coal bunkers looked rather bare. They had narrow chimneys and the dome set well forward on the boiler top.

After the line became the Wirral Railway, E.G. Barker, the Locomotive Superintendent ordered a further locomotive from Beyer, Peacock & Company. This was a 4-4-2 Tank, Wirral No.1 which had inside cylinders 16 x 24inches and 5ft 2inch coupled wheels. As built the engine had the somewhat (by that time) archaic feature of a sloping smokebox front (as also did the 0-4-4 Tanks) but received a new boiler and other modifications in 1914 resulting in a much improved appearance enhanced by coal rails on the bunker. This engine was allocated the number 6830 in the LMS list, which it never carried, being withdrawn early in 1924.

In 1894 two further engines, surprisingly a reversion to 0-4-4 type, were designed by Mr. Barker and built by Beyer, Peacock & Company. These, numbered 7 and 10 had inside cylinders measuring 17 x 24inches and 5ft 2inch coupled wheels. They were larger than their predecessors of the same wheel arrangement and even more "top-heavy" looking. Both were broken up in 1924 and never carried the LMS numbers allotted to them (6774 and 6775 respectively).

In 1896 Mr. Barker introduced a locomotive with a wheel arrangement entirely new to Britain, a 4-4-4 or "double-ender" Tank with inside cylinders 17 x 24inches and 5ft 2inch diameter coupled wheels. Built by Beyer, Peacock & Company, this notable engine, No.11 had a very short coupled wheelbase to enable it to safely negotiate the curves on the Birkenhead-Bidston and Seacombe-Bidston lines, some of which were quite sharp. The 4-4-4 wheel arrangement did not become popular in Britain, only the Metropolitan, North Eastern and Midland & South Western Junction railways having examples. After a relatively short life, No.11 was taken out of passenger service in 1919 and scrapped in February, 1920 after being used for a while on permanent-way duties (as No.16).

The next new locomotives designed by Barker were of another rare wheel arrangement, being 0-6-4 Tank engines with inside cylinders measuring 18 x 26inches. The coupled wheels were 5ft 3inches, in diameter. Introduced in 1900, these two ungainly engines were built by Beyer, Peacock & Company and became Wirral Railway No's. 12 and 13. They were mostly employed on goods and shunting work and occasionally on excursions from Birkenhead to New Brighton or to Neston over the LNW/GW Joint line beyond West Kirby. Engine No.12 was withdrawn in February, 1924 whilst No.13 went in October, 1923. They were allotted the LMS numbers 6848 and 6849 respectively, but never carried these.

In 1902 Mr. Barker left the Wirral — he had brought fame of sorts to the line through the introduction of the 4-4-4 and 0-6-4 wheel arrangements. He was succeeded by T.B. Hunter, formerly of the Mersey Railway, who had the old stables of tramway days turned into a workshop, installing up-to-date equipment to allow heavy repairs to be carried out without the necessity for having locomotives returned to the makers for such attention. This work was completed in 1903, the same year in which the Mersey Railway Company changed to electric traction and could no longer deal with repairs to Wirral steam locomotives which had been the case until then. The Mersey company needed all its limited work-shop space for the maintenance of the electric rolling stock.

The year 1903 saw the arrival of two further 4-4-4 Tank locomotives similar to No.11 and also built by Beyer, Peacock & Company. These, Nos.14 and 15 had Belpaire fireboxes, a new departure for the Wirral. They had 17 x 24inch cylinders and 5ft 3inch diameter coupled wheels. Like the prototype, these two locomotives had short lives and never carried their LMS numbers (6850 and 6851 respectively) being withdrawn in 1924.

In 1913 the company again entered the second-hand market for locomotives. In that year they obtained from the London and North Western company a 4ft 6inch 2-4-2 Tank locomotive No.3608 designed by F.W Webb and built at Crewe in 1877 as a 2-4-0 Tank and converted to a 2-4-2 in 1895. This became Wirral Railway No.4 and carried that number until it was withdrawn in April, 1927. The allotted LMS number was 6758, which was never carried.

The last locomotive to be specifically built for the Wirral Railway was a large 0-4-4 Tank with Belpaire firebox, 18 x 26inch inside cylinders and 5ft 6inch coupled wheels. Numbered 3, this engine, generally considered to have been the best on the system at that time, was built by Beyer, Peacock & Company in 1914. As good as it was however, the engine had a short life, being withdrawn in 1928 after having wandered to Carlisle as LMS No.6776. It had the distinction of being the only true Wirral Railway locomotive to actually carry its post-Grouping number. The engine was overhauled at Crewe shortly after the 1923 Grouping and stood in line in the works yard in company with numerous L&NWR engines, among which it looked somewhat out of place. Very few Beyer, Peacock locomotives ever entered Crewe, the sacred sanctum of engines designed and built at the great works of Britain's largest pre-Grouping Railway system.

After the end of the 1914-18 war the Wirral company's engines were in a run-down state and it became necessary to obtain reinforcements. The London & North Western was approached once again and they sold the Wirral people three further 2-4-2 Tank engines. The first to arrive, in June, 1919 was No.969, built in 1882. It became Wirral No.11. This engine was allotted the LMS number 6759 but never carried it. About 1924 the engine was sent to Maryport, in Cumberland and was withdrawn for scrapping in April, 1927.

The next 2-4-2 Tank engine to come from Crewe was L&NWR No.889, built in 1884. Purchased in November, 1919, this engine became Wirral Railway No.16. It was allotted LMS number 6760 but never carried it. Withdrawal date was April, 1924 so it did not last long on the Wirral lines.

In July 1920 the company received on hire L&NWR No.284, the third of the 2-4-2 Tanks, which was built in 1883 and received the Wirral number 17 after they had purchased it in January, 1921. This engine became LMS No.6761 and ran until July, 1928 though it did not stay in Wirral for long after the Grouping.

The last and probably the best engine that ever migrated to the Wirral was one of the famous Aspinall 2-4-2 Tank engines from the Lancashire & Yorkshire Railway, a type very familiar on the Lancashire side of the River Mersey. The one that went to the Wirral was L&Y No.1041, built at Horwich in 1890. Added to Wirral stock in June, 1921, it received the number 6. Before leaving its parent line, rails were added to the bunker in order to increase the coal capacity. After the Grouping this popular engine became LMS No.6762 (in April, 1925), though logically it should have been 10638 in the series of numbers allotted to its numerous companions. Shortly after the Grouping this engine was transferred away from Wirral, but returned there about 1927. It left again in 1929 for Patricroft, but in 1934 it was at Warrington, then another move was made to Preston where it spent many years, working local trains, sometimes to Liverpool. The engine's usual job at Preston however, was station Pilot — it was part of the scenery there until withdrawal in February, 1952. For a time, No.6762 appeared in the splendour of Midland Red, but soon reverted to black. There is no doubt that the Wirral Railway company received an excellent locomotive in this stray from the L&Y flock and moreover, a popular one.

Most, if not all of the Wirral company's engines were well worn after the end of the first World War and upon being absorbed into the vast stock of the LMS, had scant chance of survival. Most of them, as already outlined, were withdrawn soon after the Grouping and all except No.6762 were broken up at Crewe, the latter being scrapped at Horwich, the works in which it was built, after 62 years of excellent and reliable service.

There was one memorable occasion when the Wirral company were obliged to borrow locomotives. This was back in 1902 when an unexpected crisis hit the Locomotive Department, putting all the engines out of commission for several days. A sudden increase in the hardness of the water supplied to the system from the Birkenhead Corporation at Upton necessitated mixing it with water from another source. The resultant heavy scaling of the boilers put the engines out of service and motive power had to be borrowed from the L&NWR and GW Railways to tide over the situation until their own engines could be retuned to service. The trouble was overcome by obtaining softer water from Wallasey Corporation, which came from Lake Vrynwy in Wales.

The Wirral Railway company's colour scheme for locomotives was black, with thin white, red and yellow lining. The numbers were cast on brass plates, except on one or two of the imported engines obtained after World War 1 which bore painted numerals. Buffer beams were red and some engines had their coupling rods painted in this colour. They looked smart and attractive in this livery which was not unlike that of the London & North Western Company. The crest of the Company, The Wirral Horn surrounded by the company title was carried on the cab side sheets.

Unlike some other railways that operated intensive short-distance passenger train services, the Wirral company used the vacuum brake instead of the Westinghouse compressed air brake, so that the hiss and thump of pumps was entirely absent. Each engine carried a lifting jack on its running plate, a fairly unusual practice for Britain (the London, Tilbury & Southend Railway did likewise). The Jacks were used for getting an engine back on the rails in the event of a derailment.

After the Wirral Railway had been absorbed into the LMS group some "new" motive power was drafted to the system in the shape of several ancient L&NWR 2-4-0 Tank engines — Nos.1000, 2238, 2247 and 2252, also some other L&NWR types including 0-6-0 Special Saddle Tank No.3211 and 0-6-0 "square" Tank No.3693. L&NW 0-6-2 Tank engines of both the 4ft 3inch "Coal" and "Watford" 5ft varieties also arrived along with 4ft 6inch 2-4-2 Tanks Nos.1176, 1358, 2069 and 2051. None remained for long except the "Coal Tanks" which were found suitable for the work — these were L&NW Nos.692, 1046, 1207, 2749, 2481 and LMS 7706. The Lancashire & Yorkshire was represented by the previously mentioned 2-4-2 Tank No. 6762 and also by Barton-Wright 0-6-2 Tank engines Nos.203, 251, 264, and 679.

Two L&NWR "Coal Tanks", Nos.7744 and 7759 had their side tai k widened during 1927 in order to increase their water capacity and lasted in this form until they were scrapped long after leaving the Wirral lines. One of these, No.7759 (BR 58916) finished its days as station Pilot at Birmingham New Street, its exertions of Wirral days long behind it.

The first up-to-date locomotives arrived on the Wirral lines in 1929. These were new LMS Standard Class 3F 0-6-0 Tank engines and though to all intents and purposes classed as goods engines, they were promptly put to work on the passenger trains on which they performed with considerable success, achieving a good turn of speed and keeping the exacting schedules with ease. They were simple reliable and rugged locomotives that proved a welcome addition to the ageing fleet formerly available. Examples of the "Standard Shunters" as they were known, were still to be found in Wirral until the middle 1960's, of which more later.

Commencing in 1930, the Wirral lines at long last were provided with locomotives that were completely adequate for the work and the struggling days were over. The new engines were the Class 3P 2-6-2 Tank design introduced by Sir Henry Fowler and built at Derby. A dozen or so arrived at Birkenhead North and aroused tremendous interest in the ranks of regular passengers, so advanced did they seem in comparison with the largely pre-1900 engines hitherto in use. These 2-6-2 Tank engines performed with almost complete reliability and satisfaction until the end of the steam era in March, 1938. A few of the later (1935) Stanier 2-6-2 Tank engines with tapered boilers appeared from time to time during 1936-8 but none were permanently allocated to Birkenhead North, those used being borrowed usually from Chester depot while the native engines were away for overhaul etc.

Strangely enough the 0-4-4 wheel arrangment returned to the Wirral lines in the early 1930's — new engines at that! Three of the Stanier 0-4-4 Tanks of 1932 design built at Derby, Nos.6405, 6406 and 6407 were sent to Birkenhead, Mollington Street, but spent a great deal of their time working from Birkenhead North on the Wirral section.

By 1932 North Shed possessed only three types of locomotive — LMS Standard Class 3P 2-6-2 Tank, Class 3F 0-6-0 Tank (Standard Shunters) and L&NWR 0-6-2 "Coal Tank", all other types having been disposed of, and the three above-mentioned classes kept the services going until electrification (with assistance at times from the borrowed 0-4-4 Tank engines).

Occasionally larger locomotives visited Birkenhead North shed. One such stranger was a former Midland Class 2P 4-4-0, No.421 which was stored there for some weeks during the winter of 1937-8. Another was Stanier 2-6-0 No.2954, which was employed on the haulage of the Engineer's inspection train on 14th December, 1937 when electrification work was well advanced. Visits by any but Tank locomotives always aroused widespread interest on the LMS, but Bidston, L&NER shed had daily visits by large freight locomotives, though these did not normally venture onto LMS rails.

Upon the introduction of electric trains on the lines between Birkenhead Park, West Kirby and New Brighton on Sunday, 13th March, 1938, most of the steam locomotives were sent elsewhere. The only exceptions were four Class 3F 0-6-0 Tank engines. Nos.7353, 7503, 7504 and 7507, which were retained for local goods traffic and shunting duties, and as Birkenhead North shed was now closed the engines were allocated to Birkenhead Mollington Street depot, though stabled at the L&NER shed at Bidston. For years afterwards however, they visited the site of their former home to take on water and have their fires cleaned. The disused engine shed was demolished in 1941.

Saturday, 12th March, 1938 was the last day of steam operation on the Wirral lines and at the end of their day's work instead of leaving the coaches at the various accustomed locations and proceeding to North depot for the night, the locomotives, complete with trains proceeded instead to West Kirby at which place they left their native

63

heath and travelled to various planned destinations over the LMS/GW "Joint" line via Hooton. Probably never in all its long history had this single line, largely rural branch witnessed the passage of so many trains during a single night! In some cases the departing trains had two or even three engines in order to complete the transfer quickly, whilst some engines ran light singly or coupled together.

The last public service steam train was the 11.30 p.m. from Birkenhead Park to New Brighton with 0-6-0 Tank engine No.7503 and after this had departed 15 minutes behind schedule, silence settled over the deserted engine shed and the railway that had known steam locomotives for nearly 80 years. The engines went to other sheds, as far away as Rugby, Stoke, Llandudno and Chester.

During the final days of steam traction on the Wirral line, the train service were operated by 22 locomotives, as follows:

LMS   Standard 2-6-2 Tank Nos.2,3,4,5,12,42,44,48,49,50,51, 55 and 70.
LMS   Standard 0-6-0 Tank Nos. 7353,7503,7504,7507.
L&NWR   0-6-2 "Coal Tank" Nos. 7711,7759,7780,7841,27664.

Although the local passenger services were taken over by electric trains, one solitary steam passenger turn remained, the New Brighton-London through coaches, and these were hauled by one of the Class 3F 0-6-0 Tank engines. This useful service commenced on 1st October, 1923 with a train in each direction. The coaches were hauled to Hooton (via West Kirby) and at that place were added to a Birkenhead-Crewe train. On arrival at Crewe they were transferred to a main-line express train bound for London. The reverse proceedure was of course, followed in the opposite direction. On its inaugural journey the train consisted of three coaches and was hauled to Chester by ex-L&NWR 5ft 0-6-2 Tank locomotive No.1032, which, for a period thereafter shared the work with the ex-L&Y 2-4-2 Tank No.6762.

When the service commenced the train left New Brighton at 9.58 a.m. arriving at London, Euston at 3.10 p.m. The opposite working left Euston at 5.20 p.m., arriving at New Brighton at 10.26 p.m. The timings remained similar until the service was withdrawn upon the outbreak of the war in September, 1939. It has never been reinstated and indeed could not be resumed in the future, for the track it traversed between West Kirby and Hooton has long been removed. The trains called at Moreton, Meols, Hoylake and West Kirby ("Joint" station) in both directions.

Considerable interest was attached to the London working in latter days as it provided the rare instance of what was, to all intents and purposes, a shunting engine hauling a semi-express passenger train, as the LMS Class 3F 0-6-0 Tank engines took over. These engines were also employed, before World War 2 put an end to such things, on excursion trains between Hooton and New Brighton and vice-versa. One such train was double-headed on one memorable occasion by an 0-6-0 Tank and a former Lancashire & Yorkshire 0-6-0 goods engine running with the tender leading. It was extremely rare for other than tank locomotives to traverse former Wirral metals, so that the 0-6-0 was a real stranger.

Goods trains between Hooton and Birkenhead via West Kirby were usually worked by the LMS 0-6-0 Tank engines but after the formation of British Railways in January, 1948, former Great Western 0-6-0 Pannier Tank engines began to share in this work, providing the rare sight (except for the water-emergency of 1902) of Great Western locomotives at places such as Hoylake and Bidston. There was however one daily goods train with a GWR engine in pre-Grouping days. Workings of such engines became common during the 1950's. Other strangers appeared from time to time, such as a former L&NER Class J.94 0-6-0 Saddle Tank (No.68030) on a Birkenhead-West Kirby goods train one day in August, 1952. More interesting still, former Great Central 2-8-0 locomotives Nos.63716 and 63773 worked on permanent-way trains between Bidston and Leasowe on 26th October, 1952.

As mentioned previously, excursion trains were run to New Brighton from various places in the Midlands and elsewhere and these continued well into the diesel era. For instance, on 6th June, 1965 an eight-coach excursion from Leicester was hauled as far as Bidston by diesel-electric locomotive No.D5394. Here a steam locomotive, 2-6-4 Tank No.42086 took the train onto New Brighton and hauled it back to Bidston in the evening. The steam locomotive was required because the running-round loops at New Brighton could not accomodate a lengthy diesel locomotive. On Sunday, 27th June, 1965 an eight-coach excursion from Rugby got through to New Brighton with diesel-electric locomotive No.D5007 and owing to the fact that it could not run round the train, the latter had to be shunted by steam 2-6-4 Tank engine No.42597 which was sent specially for the job. August Bank Holiday, 1965 saw three steam locomotives on Wrexham-New Brighton trains, namely ex-Great Western 0-6-0 Pannier Tanks Nos.4683 and 9630 and BR 4-6-0 No.75012.

Recollecting the steam days in Wirral is a nostalgic exercise — the mind fills with memories of 2-6-2 Tank engines with clanking rods echoing musically across the fields and the sharp barks as they accelerated their trains of red-liveried coaches from rest at the many stations; of the scents of hot oil and coal smoke, the strong smell of creosote from the track on warm summer days and the scents of the countryside — grass, hay, gorse and wild flowers, all these intermingling to create an unforgettable picture on the mind's screen of days now long gone. Memories return too, of the off-beat sounds of the carriage wheels as they hammered their way along the short rails, of the short bursts of speed here and there, especially on the last stretch into Seacombe past the gas works, the clanking rods of the engine resounding in the cuttings and how, if one risked leaning from the carriage window the locomotive itself could be watched traversing the curves, its assembly of rods and cranks whirling in fascinating motion. One also recalls the hard pull on the last stage of the run into New Brighton with the open sea in view and distant panorama of the Lancashire coast and passing ships, the constant procession of trains through Bidston packed with people going to Moreton or West Kirby on sunny summer days. Electrification work was viewed with mixed feelings by those with an affection for the Wirral steam trains — it was more than 30 years since any other steam-operated line on Merseyside had been converted. Today such work would be hailed with pleasure as it would indicate indefinite survival and continued usefulness instead of the doubtful future of many lines worked by diesel power.

The new rolling stock for the electrified line began to arrive at Birkenhead North car sheds during 1937, the modern, gleaming vehicles making a sharp contrast with the ageing steam hauled coaches, most of which were of pre-1923 vintage though in good condition. The new trains were built by the Birmingham Railway Carriage & Wagon Company at Saltley and by the Metropolitan Cammell Carriage & Wagon Company of Smethwick. The fleet consisted of 19 three-car trains each comprising a motor, trailer and driving trailer, all of the "open" or saloon type, with steel bodies and timber interior panelling. Two sets of air-operated sliding doors were provided on either side of each vehicle. The seats in these cars, which are still in service, are arranged in similar fashion to London "underground" cars. Each motor unit has four 135 horsepower motors making for rapid acceleration and a maximum speed of 50 miles per hour, although the closely spaced stations, at which all trains call, preclude runs of any length at this speed. The outer ends of the motor and driving trailer cars are equipped with centre automatic couplings whilst buffer and screw couplings are fitted to the inner ends and to the trailer cars. All sets are close-coupled and two three-car sets are used together to form six-car trains, reduced to three-car formations in non-peak periods.

For a month or two both electric and steam trains could be seen together on the Wirral lines, due to the fact that the new trains had to be tested and former steam locomotive drivers trained as motormen. New sets were stored at West Kirby sidings and elsewhere awaiting the day of the great change-over.

The pattern of train services altered somewhat with the electrification — it was no longer necessary for passengers to change trains at Birkenhead Park. The LMS trains now worked through to Liverpool Central via the Mersey Railway, the large American type trains of the latter system running to New Brighton. On Sunday mornings however, Mersey trains ran to West Kirby and LMS trains to Rock Ferry. The whole atmosphere of the system changed overnight, the railway becoming akin to any London electric surburban line. Station porters no longer had to perform the age-old ritual of walking towards the head of each train, closing compartment doors and collecting tickets from passengers at the same time and after ascertaining that all was in order, give the guard the 'tip' by raising the right arm. From then on the train doors have been controlled automatically by means of push-buttons in the guard's compartment, though the old Mersey trains retained their barn-like manual doors.

The official "last steam train" ran on Monday, 14th March, 1938 and consisted of five new steel First Class main-line corridor coaches which, as regular passengers observed, were a considerable advance on those in which they had made their daily journeys! But — this was a VIP special! The train, with Stanier 2-6-2 Tank locomotive No.200 at the head, had arrived at Birkenhead North on the Sunday afternoon, after all the regular engines had departed. The handsome, highly polished train of red-liveried coaches conveyed Sir Joshia Stamp (President of the LMS), various other high officers of the company together with local dignitaries on a ceremonial journey from Birkenhead Park to West Kirby. It is amusing to recall that the steam locomotive was of contemporary construction with electric trains which had come to replace "old-fashioned" steam traction! At West Kirby the party changed to an electric train for the return journey through to Liverpool Central, Low Level station, whilst the steam train departed for Chester empty, via the West Kirby-Hooton Branch.

Engine No.200 was stationed at Chester when new, but was soon afterwards sent to Scotland where it continued in service throughout the war. In 1951-2 it was employed in banking service on the former Highland Railway line at Blair Athol. In 1961 No.200 was placed in storage along with many other steam locomotives at Bo'ness, and languished there for many months. It was hauled to Polmont in due course, then finally sent to Calder in October, 1963, to be broken up at the premises of J.H. Cornell, along with other members of the class.

The formation of British Railways on 1st January, 1948 brought about little alteration but it was not long before the trains began to exchange their LMS red livery for the green which the new administration adopted for electric trains, and station buildings and signal boxes were repainted in the red and cream of the London Midland Region of which the Wirral lines were now a constituent. Station signs and notices were removed and replaced by enamelled metal substitutes which were far from as durable as their predecessors, as the weather dealt severely with them. Commencing in 1966, the trains began to be repainted in the standard blue livery of British Rail, and more recently they have received blue and grey livery.

The first major change came in 1956 when the original Mersey Railway trains began to be replaced by new rolling stock. During that year and the first part of 1957, 24 three-car train sets of similar design to those introduced by the LMS were built by the same manufacturers that supplied the sets of 1938, which had, and continued to give, reliable and trouble-free service, and although there was some mild surprise expressed by passengers concerning the building of new rolling stock to a 16-years old design, the exacting nature of the traffic demanded the use of well-tried equipment and certainly the latter-day rolling stock has given no cause for dissatisfaction operation-wise. The interior appointments of the 1956 trains differed from those of the earlier vehicles in the use of plastics for panelling instead of wood veneers as formerly used in LMS passenger vehicles of the late 1930's.

All the electric motor coaches and driving trailer cars have centre automatic couplings, so that they are incompatible with stock fitted with screw couplings, although this type is disappearing nowadays. So that the trains could be taken to the main works at Horwich, near Bolton, adaptor vehicles had to be employed, one at either end of a set destined for the works. These had a screw coupling at one end and an automatic coupling at the other. An ordinary locomotive hauled the trains to and from Horwich. For a time two old ex-Midland Railway six-wheeled passenger brake vans were used as adaptor vehicles. These were later superseded by ordinary open merchandise wagons. Nowadays specially built adaptor vehicles are used, also ex-LMS long goods brake vans. The journey to Horwich was made via West Kirby, Hooton, Ellesmere Port and Warrington. Closure of the Hooton-West Kirby Branch meant the re-routing of the trains so that they now go via Bidston, the ex-Great Central line to Chester thence to Warrington and so on to Bolton etc.

By the early 1980's the 1938 trains, which had put in over 40 years of sterling service were becoming due for replacement. By this time British Rail had evolved standard types of multiple-unit electric trains, and the type chosen for the Wirral Lines was Class 508 which were at first delivered to the Southern Region for use in the London district, but proved unsuitable for longer-distance surburban service. Each train consisted of four cars, of the open saloon type, two motor and two trailer cars. The motor units are equipped with four 110 horse-power motors and are thus not as powerful as the existing Wirral Line trains although they will be adequate for the work demanded. Air suspension incorporated in the bogies makes for smooth and quieter riding, but the interior arrangements are far inferior to that of the old trains, on which almost every seat is adjacent to the wide-view window. The two and three-aside seating in the new trains, for the most part give the passengers a restricted view, as few of them are directly in line with a window, and this detracts somewhat from their popularity. The same applies to the similar trains on the Southport and Ormskirk lines. The original four-car formation has been reduced to three for Merseyrail service.

The Class 508 trains began to arrive in 1982 and it seemed strange to see vehicles with their numbers prefixed by S (for Southern) instead of the long familiar M (London Midland). Replacement of the ex-LMS trains was scheduled to commence early in 1984, followed by the 1956 BR trains, the ex-Southern trains being stored, used for driver training or putting in some service on the Liverpool side of the Mersey. Two sets were on The Southport, Ormskirk and Garston lines during 1983.

Birkenhead North workshops got a great deal of extra work in March, 1970, when Meols Cop works, Southport was closed down and trains from the Southport and Ormskirk lines were brought all the way over the Mersey for attention (except for major overhauls which continued to be carried out at Horwich). The sets, hauled by diesel locomotives travelled via Bootle Junction, the Bootle Branch to Edge Hill, thence via Olive Mount Junction to Earlestown, Warrington, Helsby, Chester, the ex-Great Central line to Bidston, thence to Birkenhead North. Since May, 1977 they have taken the short cut provided by the connection between the Southport line and the former Mersey Railway line below Lord Street, Liverpool, a section of the Mersey Railway that was no longer used for passenger traffic after the Loop Line was built.

Physical changes on the Wirral Lines since Nationalisation have included the improvement of various stations in minor ways, such as provision of illuminated train destination indicators at Birkenhead Park and North stations, and various track alterations at these two stations. On the debit side, closure of all goods and coal sidings took place as a result of the "Beeching Plan" and by the end of 1965 all Wirral line stations lost their freight facilities. The track was removed from most of the yards. Domestic coal traffic has, since 1966, been dealt with at a bulk coal depot that was established on the site of the former steam locomotive depot at Birkenhead North. Local goods traffic is non-existent these days.

Wirral Railway No.11. This is ex-L&NWR 2-4-2 Tank engine No.969, which later became LMS 6759. Built at Crewe in 1882, it lasted until 1927. Photographed near Birkenhead North shortly before the Wirral passed into the LMS system. (Photo: J. Ward collection).

Mainstay of the Wirral line services in LMS days were the standard 2-6-2 Tank engines designed by Sir Henry Fowler. No.3 of the Class is seen near its home depot at Birkenhead North in June, 1936. (Photo: W. Potter).

Primitive lifting facilites at Birkenhead North engine shed. LM&SR 2-6-2 Tank No.48 stands beneath the sheer-legs, October, 1937. (Photo: F. Hewitt).

Wagons in Bidston station yard, September, 1964 when the rural scene still remained. (Photo: J.W. Gahan).

A train occupies the last surviving siding at Hoylake, in July 1983. The expanse of bare ground between the main line and fence marks the site of two other sidings which existed here until recently. (Photo: S.G. Jones).

Passengers entraining at West Kirby station in May, 1983. The modern platform canopy contrasts with the original main buildings which still survive.
(Photo: S.G. Jones).

The Train Services

Next for consideration, rather briefly, are the train services on the Wirral Railway. We have already seen that the initial service of six trains in each direction on weekdays between Birkenhead and Hoylake were considered sufficient in 1866. Sparse as this service was, it became worse shortly afterwards! In 1869 there were only five trains in each direction. Two of these were described in "Bradshaw" as "Government Trains", (9.05 a.m. Birkenhead to Hoylake and 2.20 p.m. Hoylake-Birkenhead). On Sundays only three trains were provided each way. By the late 1880's 22 trains were operated in each direction between Birkenhead Park and West Kirby, with eight each way on Sundays. By the time of the 1914 war the weekday service had increased to about 40 trains in each direction, but the Sunday service remained unchanged from that of the 1880's. In the Summer of 1937, the last year of steam operation a generally half-hourly service was operated on weekdays, with an hourly service in the late evenings, but extra trains were run during peak hours for business people and workmen. On Sundays about 40 trains were operated in each direction, but this service was augmented if demand arose.

On the Birkenhead-New Brighton line the service at the time of the first World War was aproximately 37 trains in each direction on weekdays but only eight on Sundays — the latter was rather poor for an up-and-coming seaside resort. In 1937, the last year of steam working a 20-minute service was provided throughout the main part of the day, with additional peak-period trains. The Sunday service consisted of a train in each direction about every 20 minutes for most of the day, but in high Summer this was considerably increased if passenger totals were heavy.

The Seacombe Branch had about 17 trains in each direction, to and from West Kirby in the immediate period before the first World War, the Sunday service consisting of eight trains in each direction. By the Summer of 1937 the service (the last one under steam traction), had become one of about 20 trains in each direction on weekdays and a Sunday service almost as frequent.

The electric train service between Liverpool, Central station and West Kirby consisted of a train in each direction every 15 minutes for most of the day and every 10 minutes in the morning and evening peak traffic periods. The Saturday service was similar but with the 10-minute service for two morning periods — early on, and around mid-day to cater for workers who had a half-day holiday on Saturdays. The Sunday service provided a train every half-hour, but this was increased considerably during the Summer season. In 1973 the weekday service was a train every 20 minutes (10 minutes in peak hours). On Saturdays a 20-minute service was operated throughout the whole day. On Sundays there was a train every 20 minutes for most of the day. By 1983 a 15-minute service operated after the morning peak, until the evening rush period when it was increased to a 10-minute frequency, then every 20 minutes until late evening. On Saturdays the frequencies were slightly different. Sunday services were standardised at 30 minutes throughout most of the day, Summer and Winter alike.

The 1938 service on the New Brighton line gave a train every 15 minutes Monday to Friday, with 10-minute rush-hour frequencies, the Saturday service being generally similar. There was a 15-minute service on Sundays, increased during the Summer Season as demand warranted. In 1973 the Monday-Friday service was at 20-minute intervals, 10 minutes in Peak periods, but on Saturdays a 20-minute service operated for most of the day. On Sundays the service was every 30 minutes for most of the day. There were no Summer-time extras. The 1983 services on weekdays, Saturdays and Sundays corresponded closely to those on the West Kirby line.

What does the future hold for the remaining lines of the former Wirral Railway? In an era that has witnessed the wholesale closure of branch, connecting and secondary lines — and some main lines, the Wirral system has held its own and increased its traffic, though running at a loss nowadays. The Wirral Peninsula has developed enormously as a residential dormitory area for Liverpool and Birkenhead this process having started long before the Second World War. Competition was provided as far back as the 1920's by numerous bus services that quickly spread throughout Wirral, but the trains continued to do good business. The once popular and busy resort of New Brighton, to which the railway carried thousands of visitors during the summer has become mainly a residential town since the last war, so commuter traffic has to a great extent replaced the holiday traffic, whilst vastly fewer numbers of day trippers travel to Moreton or West Kirby by train, again commuter traffic being the chief function of the railway nowadays. The lines have been grant-aided for some years, but their retention and development is certain, because they are vital to the commerce of Merseyside with their enormous daily passenger totals that no other means of transport could deal with so expeditiously.

The Wirral train services have been operated under the direction of the Merseyside Passenger Transport Executive since 1st January, 1970 but the physical plant and the rolling stock remain under the control of British Railways. The policy of the MPTE is to improve and to integrate bus and train services and a great deal in this direction was accomplished in a very short time after the organisation had begun to function.

In 1971 the Mersey and Wirral lines, together with the Liverpool-Southport and Ormskirk lines, plus certain local services to and from

Lime Street were given the collective title Merseyrail, and schemes were inaugurated to radically improve the system. So far as the Wirral section is concerned, the most momentous event has been the construction of the Liverpool Loop Line, an underground extension of the Mersey Railway, over which the Wirral trains operate. This was opened to traffic in May, 1977. As the tunnel is single-tracked, it was necessary to provide gangway communication throughout each train, this work commencing in August, 1972.

Considerable alterations to Birkenhead Park station took place during 1972-3 to allow for the operation of an additional train service from and back to the station via the Loop, so as to give a more frequent service between Birkenhead and Liverpool, supplementary to the longer-distance trains. The two tracks between the island platforms were removed and the platforms merged into one except for a bay formed at the East end to accomodate the short service. The latter did not materialise however, so the platforms were separated again and the single bay line extended to make a through line, resulting in the somewhat unusual arrangement of allowing access either side of a train, but this is not practiced, however. A loop line on the North side of the station lasted until May, 1983, when it was removed. Much other track was removed from Park station under the 1972 scheme.

Birkenhead North station had its track and signalling arrangements considerably modified during 1970 to accomodate the diesel M.U. trains on the Wrexham service, which were transferred there from New Brighton on 4th January, 1971, but continued to serve New Brighton on Sundays. This arrangement lasted until 11th January, 1976 when the Sunday trains also were transferred to North. More recently the service was cut back to Bidston. Instead of four lines passing through the station there are now only two, serving the side platform and South face of the island, whilst a loop and one dead-end siding are provided on the North side of the island platform. At the West end sidings and connections are provided to serve the electric train maintenance depot which lies to that end of the station beyond Stanley Road Bridge.

No further major works took place on the Wirral line until 1983, when, in preparation for the introduction of Class 508 electric train sets, transferred from the Southern Region, to replace the 1938 and 1956 trains, the platforms of various stations were lengthened. At the same time the Birkenhead North maintenance depot was extended, the layout and signalling re-modelled, and a new washing plant and staff accomodation provided. This depot has undertaken repairs to Southport line trains for a number of years in addition to dealing with their own Wirral trains. The Class 508 trains began to arrive in 1982, as mentioned earlier.

75

"This is the age of the train" was the slogan of the early 1980's, a welcome change from the run-down of railways and bus services that has taken place over the last 30 years. It is pleasing indeed to see that this trend has been halted on Merseyside, and schemes mooted long ago and repeatedly shelved, having at last become a reality. It is even more pleasing to see the lines of the old Wirral Railway playing an important role in the passenger transport of the 1980's. Braithwaite Poole would be delighted indeed, could he see how his small single line "railway over the sand" has developed into a busy and vital line of communication of immense value to the communities on both sides of that once great divide, the River Mersey, now completely conquered.

The bland face of an ex-LM&S design train contrasts with the "goo-goo" eyed look of a modern Class 508 unit at Birkenhead North in 1983. The latter type of train is destined to take over Wirral line services in 1984 (Photo: S.G. Jones).

A Merseyrail train departing from Bidston in September, 1983. Iron ore conveyors and the chimney of the new refuse incinerator form the background. (Photo: S.G. Jones).

The level crossing at Leasowe station with road traffic halted while a Liverpool-bound train passes. July, 1983. (Photo: S.G. Jones).

Milcage Table

WEST KIRBY - BIRKENHEAD PARK

West Kirby	0	miles
Hoylake	$1\frac{1}{4}$	miles
Manor Road	$1\frac{3}{4}$	miles
Meols	$2\frac{1}{2}$	miles
Moreton	$4\frac{1}{4}$	miles
Leasowe	5	miles
Bidston	$5\frac{3}{4}$	miles
Birkenhead North	$6\frac{3}{4}$	miles
Birkenhead Park	$7\frac{3}{4}$	miles

NEW BRIGHTON - BIRKENHEAD PARK

New Brighton	0	miles
Wallasey, Grove Road	$1\frac{1}{4}$	miles
Wallasey Village	$\frac{1}{2}$	miles
Birkenhead North	$3\frac{1}{4}$	miles
Birkenhead Park	$4\frac{1}{4}$	miles

SEACOMBE & EGREMONT - BIDSTON

Seacombe & Egremont	0	miles
Liscard & Poulton	$1\frac{1}{2}$	miles
Bidston	3	miles

SPECIAL STAMP FOR NEWS CORRESPONDENCE
WIRRAL RAILWAY COMPANY
2d.
CARRIED AT OWNERS RISK
COLLECTION ON DELIVERY NOT INCLUDED
TO BE CALLED FOR BY CONSIGNEE AT THE STATION TO WHICH IT IS ADDRESSED
THE COMPANY RESERVE THE RIGHT OF OPENING AND SURCHARGING IF INSUFFICIENTLY STAMPED

ACKNOWLEDGEMENTS

The following sources were of valuable assistance in the preparation of this book: The Journal of the Stephenson Locomotive Society; "The Wirral Railway" by C. Highet (The Oakwood Press); "The Rise and Progress of Wallasey" (Wallasey Corporation); The Railway Magazine; The Railway World; The Porcupine; Bradshaw's Railway Guide. For the supply of illustrations I am indebted to P. Bates, F. Hewitt, M. Jenkins, S.G. Jones, W. Potter, G. Rose, J. Ryan and J. Ward. Unfortunately the origins of some of the older photographs are difficult to trace, but I am thankful that the photographers concerned were on the scene to record things now passed into history. Patricia Shimmin graciously volunteered to type the manuscript. My best thanks to all the above named for their interest and help.

Liverpool.
September, 1983.

79

WIRRAL RAILWAY CIRCLE

The Wirral Railway Circle was founded by a group of Merseyside railway enthusiasts in October 1968 when it seemed that the passing of steam traction on British Rail had left behind a vacuum in railway interest. The varied programme of outdoor visits, indoor meetings and regular publication of the Circle Journal which evolved in the early years has continued since. Until 1979, an attractive series of day and weekend railtours was successfully promoted but a marked increase in tour charges together with reduced support and other factors has regrettably led to their cessation for the present.

Our meetings are normally held on the second Tuesday of each month from September to May at the Williamson Art Gallery and Museum, Slatey Road, Birkenhead at 19.30 hours, when invited speakers deal with a wide range of railway and associated transport topics. However, one evening is reserved for members to show their own slides and films. The Circle boasts a valuable library whose books may be borrowed for a small fee.

Members are encouraged to submit articles and news items for the WRC Journal which is published with photographs three times a year. A membership card and attractive badge on first joining are provided while a bottle-green tie may be purchased in addition.

Interest in railways takes many diverse forms and over the years, we feel a friendly spirit has emerged through our various fixtures, encouraging these interests to develop and we invite you to join us too as a member. The membership year commences on 1st January but applications received on or after 1st April or on or after 1st August are accepted at $\frac{2}{3}$rds and $\frac{1}{3}$rd of the annual rate respectively. Reduced subscriptions are available for younger members and senior citizens.

More details can be obtained by sending a stamped addressed envelope to: A.M. Rodgers, WRC Secretary, 43, Springfield Avenue, Newton, West Kirby, Wirral, Merseyside. L48 9XB.